Images from the Region of the Pueblo Indians of North America

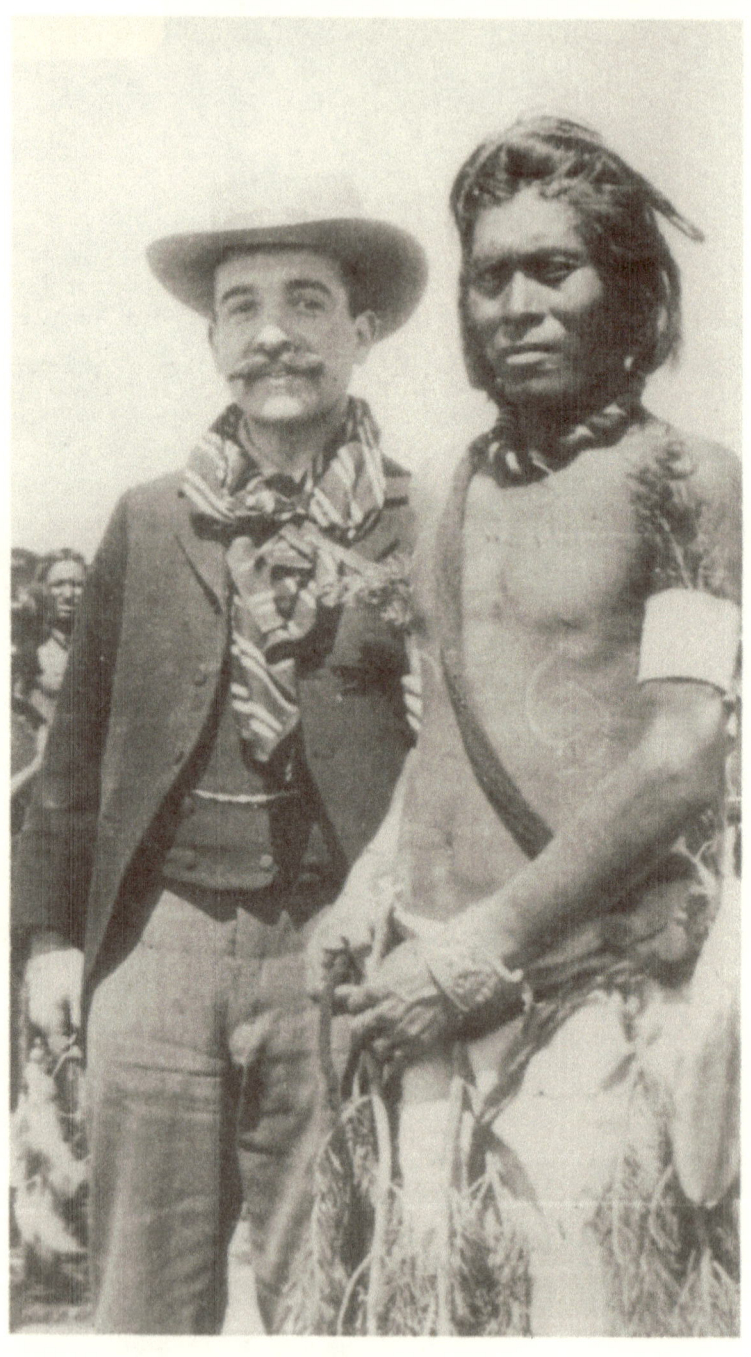

IMAGES
from the Region
of the Pueblo Indians
of North America

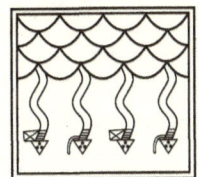

ABY M. WARBURG

Translated with an interpretive essay by
MICHAEL P. STEINBERG

CORNELL UNIVERSITY PRESS

Ithaca and London

The translation of *Bilder aus dem Gebiet der Pueblo-Indianer in Nord-Amerika* is published by arrangement with the Warburg Institute, University of London.

Copyright © 1995 by Cornell University

First published 1995 by Cornell University Press

Printed in the United States of America

Library of Congress Cataloging-in-Publication Data

Warburg, Aby, 1866–1929.
   [Bilder aus dem Gebiet der Pueblo-Indianer in Nord-Amerika. English]
   Images from the region of the Pueblo Indians of North America /
Aby M. Warburg ; translated with an interpretive essay by
Michael P. Steinberg.
     p. cm.
   Includes bibliographical references.
   ISBN 978-0-8014-8435-3 (alk. paper).
   1. Pueblo Indians—Religion   2. Serpent worship.   I. Steinberg,
Michael P. II. Title.
E99.P9W32   1995
299'.784—dc20   95–9564

Printed in the United States of America

Contents

Prefatory Note

In Aby Warburg's "Images from the Region of the Pueblo Indians of North America" we have the transcript of a slide lecture given by a patient in Ludwig Binswanger's Kreuzlingen Sanatorium to an invited audience on 21 April 1923. The German text was edited from Warburg's final draft, in Hamburg, by Fritz Saxl and Gertrud Bing, Warburg's assistants, both of whom later served as directors of the Warburg Library and Warburg Institute. Warburg did not consider the lecture publishable. In a letter of 26 April 1923, he asked Saxl to file all the lecture material and show it to no one without his explicit approval, with the exceptions of his wife, his brother Max, and two colleagues, of whom one was Ernst Cassirer. Cassirer, he suggested, might be interested in looking further into his notes brought back from America in 1897. Beyond these modest uses, the piece was, for Warburg, a prisoner of its multiple limitations. It is, he wrote, "the gruesome convulsion of a decapitated frog," "formless and philologically unfounded," and might have value only "as a document in the history of symbolic practice."

In 1938, nine years after Warburg's death and just over four years after the Warburg Library was moved from Hamburg to London, Saxl and Bing commissioned an abridged English translation from a Cambridge

Germanist, W. F. Mainland. This was published as "A Lecture on Serpent Ritual" in the *Journal of the Warburg Institute* (2[1938–39]: 277–92). The full German text was published for the first time in 1988, under the title "Serpent Ritual: An Account of a Journey (*Schlangenritual: Ein Reisebericht,* with an afterword by Ulrich Raulff [Berlin: Klaus Wagenbach, 1988]).

As Raulff suggested in his afterword, "Aby Warburg's Kreuzlingen lecture is a structure with many entrances." The text can be read as a window on the life and work of a great European scholar. It can be read as an insightful and quirky document in the history of the ethnography of the Native American Southwest. These are, as it were, its two "subjects." At the same time, the text has its own subjectivity, its own voice, which transcends both its author and his objects of analysis. It is a voice of spiraling and endless mediation: between cultures, between pasts and presents, between the self that is known and the self that is secret.

The interpretive essay that follows Warburg's lecture is an attempt to draw out the various and overlapping hermeneutics of the text itself. Its length derives from the wish to serve Warburg's text and certainly not to overshadow it. As such, the essay continues the work of translation, which can be said to involve the reproduction of resonances.

My work on this book has been guided by a sense of dual homage: to Aby Warburg himself—to his complex, vulnerable, and humorous mind; and to Anne Marie Meyer, who has been associated with the Warburg Institute for more than half a century and whose friendship, knowledge, and criticism have been essential to me within and beyond the bounds of this project. I could not have completed the project without her; I would not have tried. The Warburg Institute's two directors during the period I have been at work, J. B. Trapp and Nicholas Mann, have been generous hosts and advisers. I am also grateful to the institute's photographic staff for their help ix on the plates, many of which required the reconstruction of worn negatives. Finally, I thank the scholars who have read, heard, and improved drafts of my essay, especially Barbara Babcock, Wendy Doniger, Hal Foster, Carlo Ginzburg, Anthony Grafton, Curtis Hinsley, Michael Ann Holly, Lutz Niethammer, and Anthony Vidler.

MICHAEL P. STEINBERG

Ithaca, New York

List of Illustrations

The majority of the photographs reproduced here were taken by Aby Warburg during his American journey in 1895 and 1896. He had the photographs from the trip made into slides, of which he showed forty-seven during his lecture of 21 April 1923. This number and the titles he gave to the photographs are evident from a typed list of slides and titles dated 18 April 1923. In the abridged version of the lecture published in the *Journal of the Warburg Institute* in 1938, twenty-seven photographs with Native American subjects (plus "Uncle Sam") were reproduced, supplemented by illustrations from the classical and European material mentioned in the final part of Warburg's lecture. The German edition of 1988 reproduced these same images with several additions. Materials held in the Warburg Archive of the Warburg Institute include numerous photographs that I believe to be among the twenty or so images that have not been reproduced since the 1923 lecture; some of these I have included here. The Warburg Archive also contains, as noted in my essay, other visual materials, such as postcards and sketches, some of which are duplicated here. The following is a list of all visual material contained in the current volume, attributed as precisely as can be.

ILLUSTRATIONS

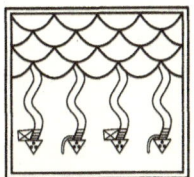

Images from the Region of the Pueblo Indians of North America

Es ist ein altes Buch zu blättern,
Athen-Oraibi, alles Vettern.

It is a lesson from an old book:
the kinship of Athens and Oraibi.

If I am to show you images, most of which I photographed myself, from a journey undertaken some twenty-seven years in the past, and to accompany them with words, then it behooves me to preface my attempt with an explanation. The few weeks I have had at my disposal have not given me the chance to revive and to work through my old memories in such a way that I might offer you a solid introduction into the psychic life of the Indians. Moreover, even at the time, I was unable to give depth to my impressions, as I had not mastered the Indian language. And here in fact is the reason why it is so difficult to work on these pueblos: Nearby as they live to each other, the Pueblo Indians speak so many and such varied languages that even American scholars have the greatest difficulty penetrating even one of them. In addition, a journey limited to several weeks could not impart truly profound impressions. If these impressions are now more blurred than they were, I can only assure you that, in sharing my distant memories, aided by the immediacy of the photographs, what I have to say will offer an impression both of a world whose culture is dying out and of a problem of decisive importance in the general writing of cultural history: In what ways can we perceive essential character traits of primitive pagan humanity?

The Pueblo Indians derive their name from their sedentary lives in villages (Spanish: *pueblos*) as opposed to the nomadic lives of the tribes who until several decades ago warred and hunted in the same areas of New Mexico and Arizona where the Pueblos now live.

What interested me as a cultural historian was that in the midst of a country that had made technological culture into an admirable precision weapon in the hands of intellectual man, an enclave of primitive pagan humanity was able to maintain itself and—an entirely sober struggle for existence notwithstanding—to engage in hunting and agriculture with an unshakable adherence to magical practices that we are accustomed to condemning as a mere symptom of a completely backward humanity. Here, however, what we would call superstition goes hand in hand with livelihood. It consists of a religious devotion to natural phenomena, to animals and plants, to which the Indians attribute active souls, which they believe they can influence primarily through their masked dances. To us, this synchrony of fantastic magic and sober purposiveness appears as a symptom of a cleavage; for the Indian this is not schizoid but, rather, a liberating experience of the boundless communicability between man and environment.

At the same time, one aspect of the Pueblo Indians' religious psychology requires that our analysis proceed with the greatest caution. The material is contaminated:

ABY M. WARBURG

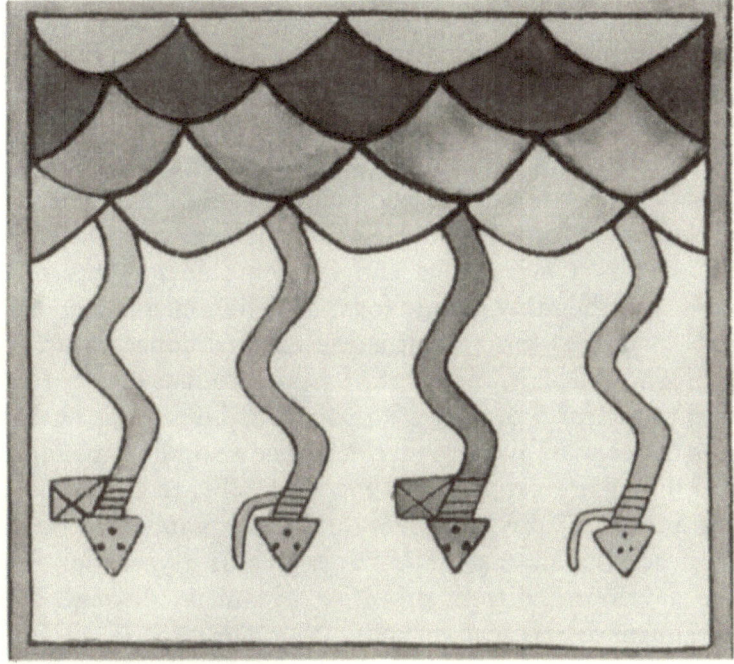

Fig. 1. Serpent as lightning.
Reproduction of an altar floor, kiva ornamentation.

it has been layered over twice. From the end of the sixteenth century, the Native American foundation was overlaid by a stratum of Spanish Catholic Church education, which suffered a violent setback at the end of the seventeenth century, to return thereafter but never officially to reinstate itself in the Moki villages. And then came the third stratum: North American education.

Yet closer study of Pueblo pagan religious formation and practice reveals an objective geographic constant, and that is the scarcity of water. For so long as the railways remained unable to reach the settlements, drought and desire for water led to the same magical practices toward the binding of hostile natural forces as they did in primitive, pretechnological cultures all over the world. Drought teaches magic and prayer.

IMAGES FROM THE REGION OF THE PUEBLO INDIANS

4 The specific issue of religious symbolism is revealed in the ornamentation of pottery. A drawing I obtained personally from an Indian will show how apparently purely decorative ornaments must in fact be interpreted symbolically and cosmologically and how alongside one basic element in cosmologic imagery—the universe conceived in the form of a house—an irrational animal figure appears as a mysterious and fearsome demon: the serpent. But the most drastic form of the animistic (i.e., nature-inspiring) Indian cult is the masked dance, which I shall show first in the form of a pure animal dance, second in the form of a tree-worshipping dance, and finally as a dance with live serpents. A glance at similar phenomena in pagan Europe will bring us, finally, to the following question: To what extent does this pagan world view, as it persists among the Indians, give us a yardstick for the development from primitive paganism, through the paganism of classical antiquity, to modern man?

All in all it is a piece of earth only barely equipped by nature, which the prehistoric and historic inhabitants of the region have chosen to call their home. Apart from the narrow, furrowing valley in the northeast, through which the Rio Grande del Norte flows to the Gulf of Mexico, the landscape here consists essentially of plateaus: extensive, horizontally situated masses of limestone and tertiary rock, which soon form higher plateaus with steep edges and smooth surfaces. (The term *mesa* compares them with tables.) These are often pierced by flowing waters, . . . by ravines and canyons sometimes a thousand feet deep and more, with walls that from their highest points plummet almost vertically, as if they had been sliced with a saw. . . . For the greater part of the year the plateau landscape remains entirely without precipitation and the vast majority of the canyons are completely dried up; only at the time that snow melts and during the brief rainy periods do powerful water masses roar through the bald ravines.[1]

ABY M. WARBURG

In this region of the Colorado plateau of the Rocky
Mountains, where the states of Colorado, Utah, New
Mexico, and Arizona meet, the ruined sites of prehistoric
communities survive alongside the currently inhabited
Indian villages. In the northwestern part of the plateau,
in the state of Colorado, are the now abandoned cliff-
dwellings: houses built into clefts of rock. The eastern
group consists of approximately eighteen villages, all
relatively accessible from Santa Fe and Albuquerque. The
especially important villages of the Zuñi lie more to the
southwest and can be reached in a day's journey from
Fort Wingate. The hardest to reach—and therefore the
most undisturbed in the preservation of ancient ways—
are the villages of the Moki (Hopi), six in all, rising out of
three parallel ridges of rock.

In the midst, in the plains, lies the Mexican settlement
of Santa Fe, now the capital of New Mexico, having
come under the dominion of the United States after a
hard struggle, which lasted into the last century. From
here, and from the neighboring town of Albuquerque,
one can reach the majority of the eastern Pueblo villages
without great difficulty.

Near Albuquerque is the village of Laguna, which,
though it does not lie quite so high as the others, provides a very good example of a Pueblo settlement. The
actual village lies on the far side of the Atchison–Topeka–Santa Fe railway line. The European settlement,
below in the plain, abuts on the station. The indigenous
village consists of two-storied houses. The entrance is
from the top: one climbs up a ladder, as there is no door
at the bottom. The original reason for this type of house
was its superior defensibility against enemy attack. In
this way the Pueblo Indians developed a cross between a
house and a fortification which is characteristic of their
civilization and probably reminiscent of prehistoric
American times. It is a terraced structure of houses
whose ground floors sit on second houses which can sit

IMAGES FROM THE REGION OF THE PUEBLO INDIANS

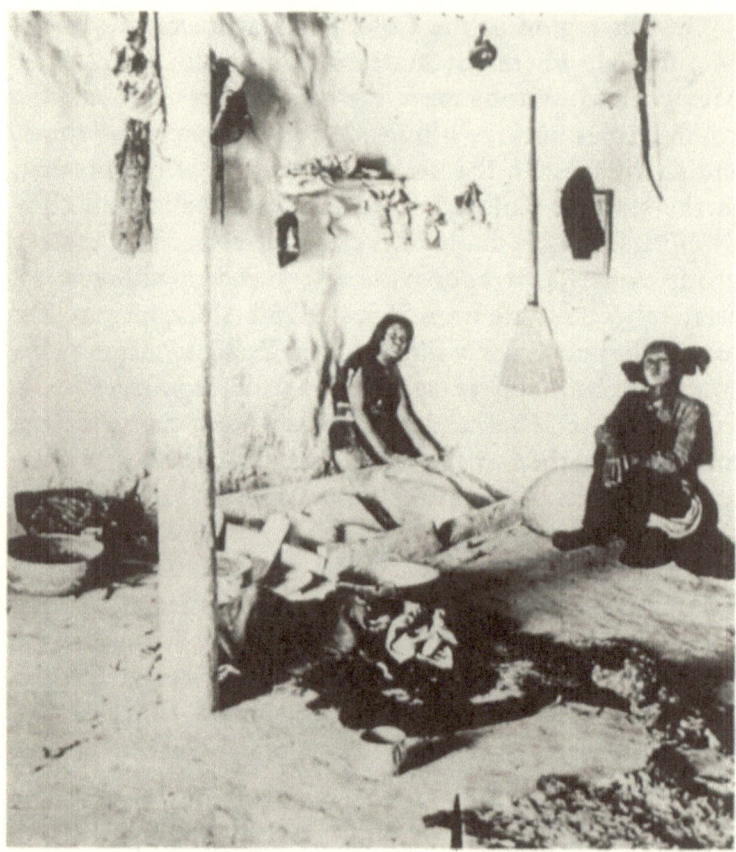

Fig. 2. Interior of a house in Oraibi with dolls and broom.
Warburg's photograph.

on yet third ones and thus form a conglomeration of rectangular living quarters.

In the interior of such a house, small dolls are suspended from the ceiling—not mere toy dolls but rather like the figures of saints that hang in Catholic farmhouses (*Figure 2*). They are the so-called kachina dolls: faithful representations of the masked dancers, the demoniac mediators between man and nature at the periodic festivals that accompany the annual harvest cycle and who constitute some of the most remarkable and unique expressions

ABY M. WARBURG

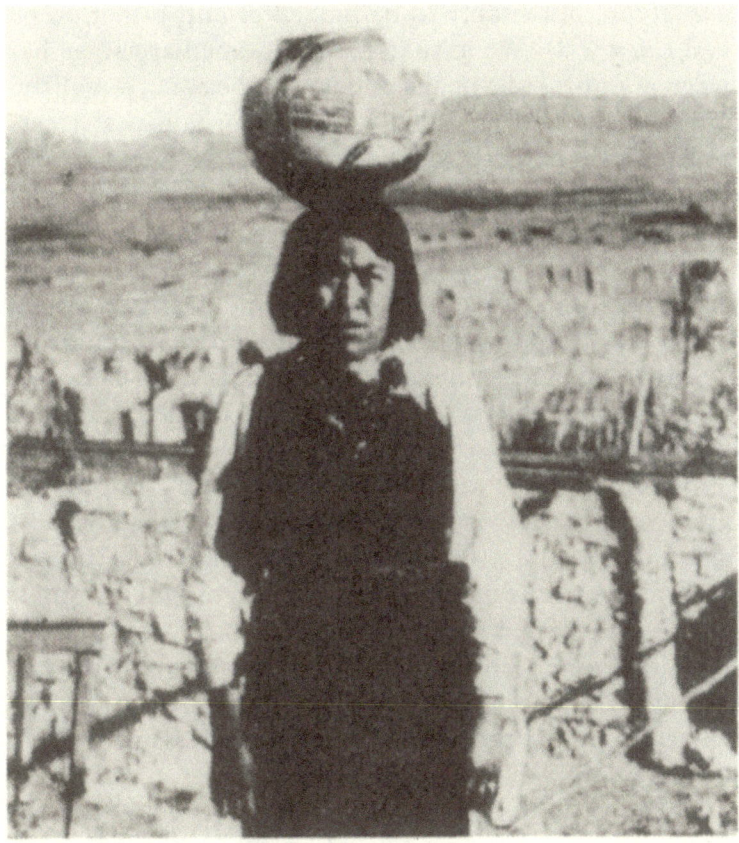

Fig. 3. Laguna. Young woman carrying a pot inscribed with bird "hieroglyph." Warburg's photograph.

of this farmers' and hunters' religion. On the wall, in contradistinction to these dolls, hangs the symbol of intruding American culture: the broom.

But the most essential product of the applied arts, with both practical and religious purposes, is the earthenware pot, in which water is carried in all its urgency and scarcity. The characteristic style for the drawings on these pots is a skeletal heraldic image. A bird, for example, may be dissected into its essential component parts to form a heraldic abstraction. It becomes a

IMAGES FROM THE REGION OF THE PUEBLO INDIANS

hieroglyph, not simply to be looked at but, rather, to be read (*Figure 3*). We have here an intermediary stage between a naturalistic image and a sign, between a realistic mirror image and writing. From the ornamental treatment of such animals, one can immediately see how this manner of seeing and thinking can lead to symbolic pictographic writing.

The bird plays an important part in Indian mythical perception, as anyone familiar with the Leatherstocking Tales knows. Apart from the devotion it receives, like every other animal, as a totem, as an imaginary ancestor, the bird commands a special devotion in the context of the burial cult. It seems even that a thieving bird-spirit belonged to the fundamental representations of the mythical fantasies of the prehistoric Sikyatki. The bird has a place in idolatrous cults for its feathers. The Indians have made a special prayer instrument out of small sticks—*bahos*; tied with feathers, they are placed on fetish altars and planted on graves. According to the authoritative explanations of the Indians, the feathers act as winged entities bearing the Indians' wishes and prayers to their demoniac essences in nature.

There is no doubt that contemporary Pueblo pottery shows the influence of medieval Spanish technique, as it was brought to the Indians by the Jesuits in the eighteenth century. The excavations of Fewkes have established incontrovertably, however, that an older potting technique existed, autonomous from the Spanish.[2] It bears the same heraldic bird motives together with the *serpent,* which for the Mokis—as in all pagan religious practice—commands cultic devotion as the most vital symbol. This serpent still appears on the base of contemporary vessels exactly as Fewkes found it on prehistoric ones: coiled, with a feathered head. On the rims, four terrace-shaped attachments carry small representations of animals. We know from work on Indian mysteries that these animals—for example, the frog and the spider—

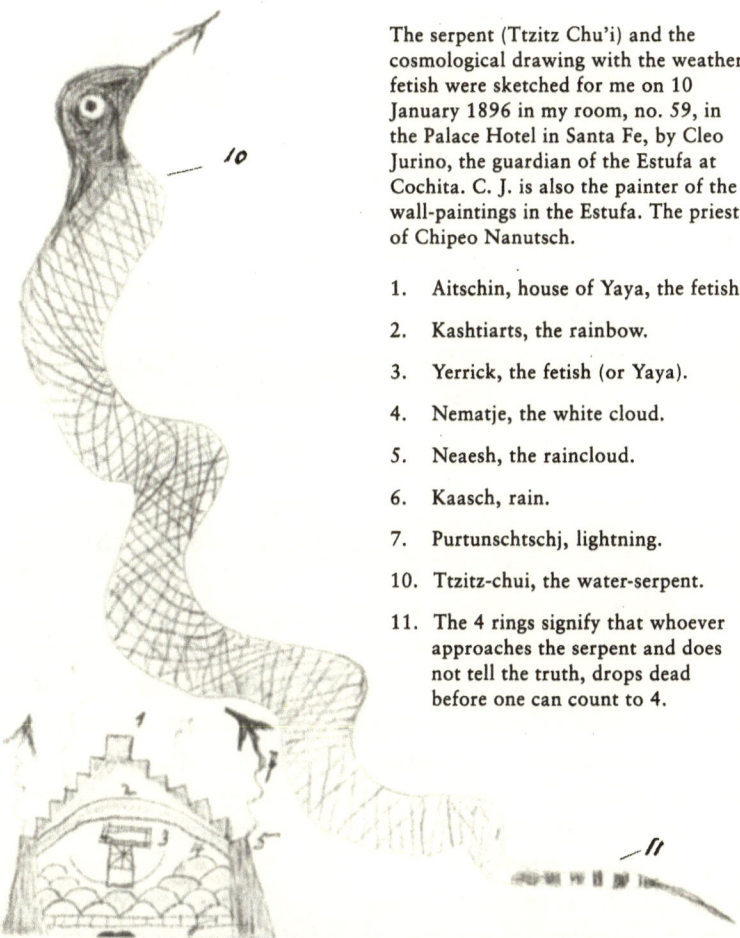

The serpent (Ttzitz Chu'i) and the cosmological drawing with the weather-fetish were sketched for me on 10 January 1896 in my room, no. 59, in the Palace Hotel in Santa Fe, by Cleo Jurino, the guardian of the Estufa at Cochita. C. J. is also the painter of the wall-paintings in the Estufa. The priest of Chipeo Nanutsch.

1. Aitschin, house of Yaya, the fetish.

2. Kashtiarts, the rainbow.

3. Yerrick, the fetish (or Yaya).

4. Nematje, the white cloud.

5. Neaesh, the raincloud.

6. Kaasch, rain.

7. Purtunschtschj, lightning.

10. Ttzitz-chui, the water-serpent.

11. The 4 rings signify that whoever approaches the serpent and does not tell the truth, drops dead before one can count to 4.

Fig. 4. Drawing by Cleo Jurino of serpent and "worldhouse," with Warburg's annotations.

represent the points of the compass and that these vessels are placed in front of the fetishes in the subterranean prayer room known as the *kiva*. In the kiva, at the core of devotional practice, the serpent appears as the symbol of lightning (*Figure 1*).

In my hotel in Santa Fe, I received from an Indian, Cleo Jurino, and his son, Anacleto Jurino, original drawings that, after some resistance, they made before my eyes

IMAGES FROM THE REGION OF THE PUEBLO INDIANS

and in which they outlined their cosmologic world view with colored pencils (*Figure 4*). The father, Cleo, was one of the priests and painter of the kiva in Cochiti. The drawing showed the serpent as a weather deity, as it happens, unfeathered but otherwise portrayed exactly as it appears in the image on the vase, with an arrow-pointed tongue. The roof of the worldhouse bears a stair-shaped gable. Above the walls spans a rainbow, and from massed clouds below flows the rain, represented by short strokes. In the middle, as the true master of the stormy worldhouse, appears the fetish (not a serpent figure): Yaya or Yerrick.

In the presence of such paintings the pious Indian invokes the storm with all its blessings through magical practices, of which to us the most astonishing is the handling of live, poisonous serpents. As we saw in Jurino's drawing, the serpent in its lightning shape is magically linked to lightning.

The stair-shaped roof of the worldhouse and the serpent-arrowhead, along with the serpent itself, are constitutive elements in the Indians' symbolic language of images. I would suggest without any doubt that the stairs contain at least a Pan-American and perhaps a worldwide symbol of the cosmos.

A photograph of the underground kiva of Sia, after Mrs. Stevenson, shows the organization of a carved lightning altar as the focal point of sacrificial ceremony, with the lightning serpent in the company of other sky-oriented symbols. It is an altar for lightning from all points of the compass. The Indians crouching before it have placed their sacrificial offerings on the altar and hold in their hand the symbol of mediating prayer: the feather (*Figure 5*).

My wish to observe the Indians directly under the influence of official Catholicism was favored by circumstance. I was able to accompany the Catholic priest Père Juillard, whom I had met on New Year's Day 1895 [*sic*]

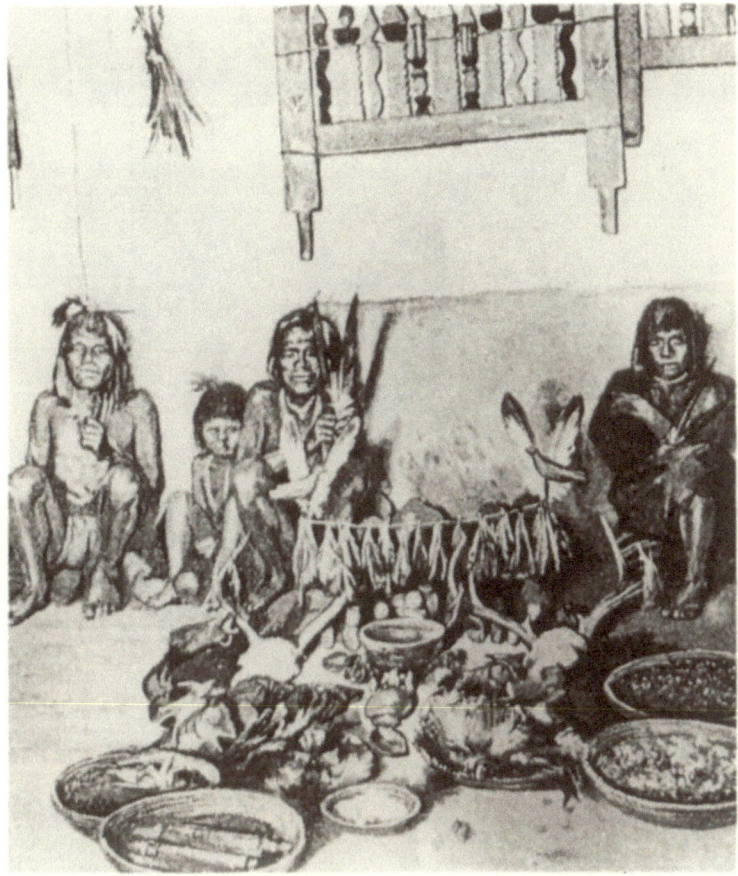

II

Fig. 5. The kiva at Sia. Interior with lightning altar (in the style of Matilda Coxe Stevenson).

while watching a Mexican Matachina dance, on an inspection tour that took him to the romantically situated village of Acoma.

We traveled through this gorse-grown wilderness for about six hours, until we could see the village emerging from the sea of rock, like a Heligoland in a sea of sand. Before we had reached the foot of the rock, bells began to ring in honor of the priest. A squad of brightly clad redskins [*Rothäute*] came running with lightning speed

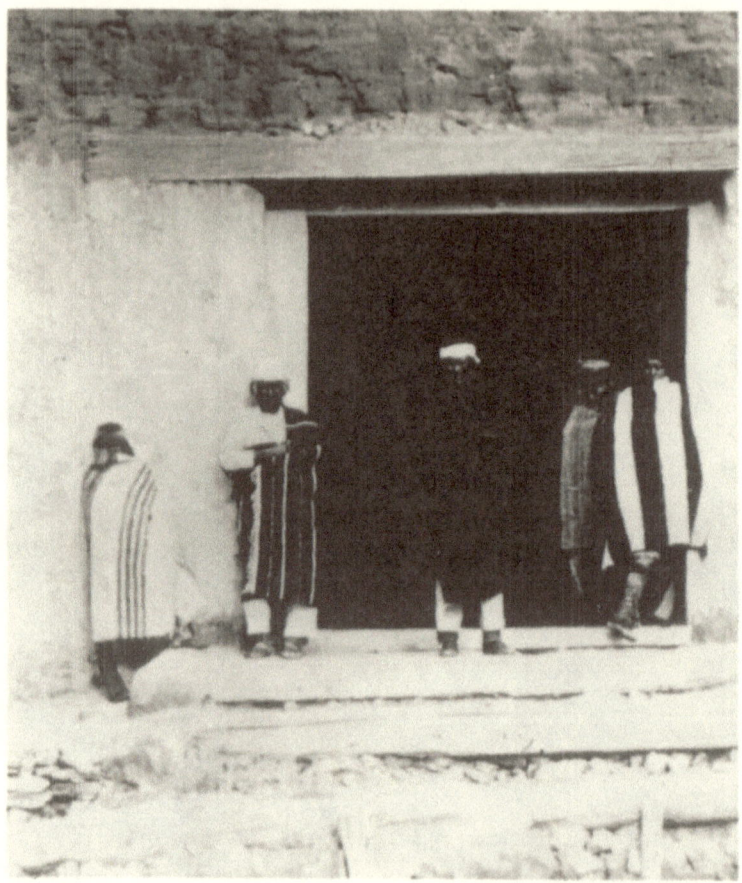

Fig. 6. In front of the Acoma church door. Warburg's photograph.

down the path to carry up our luggage. The carriages remained below, a necessity that proved ill fated: the Indians stole a cask of wine the priest had received as a gift from the nuns of Bernalillo. Once on top, we were immediately received with all the trappings of honor by the Governador—Spanish names for the ruling village chiefs are still in use. He put the priest's hand to his lips with a slurping noise, inhaling, as it were, the greeted person's aura in a gesture of reverential welcome. We were housed in his large main room together with the coachmen, and

ABY M. WARBURG

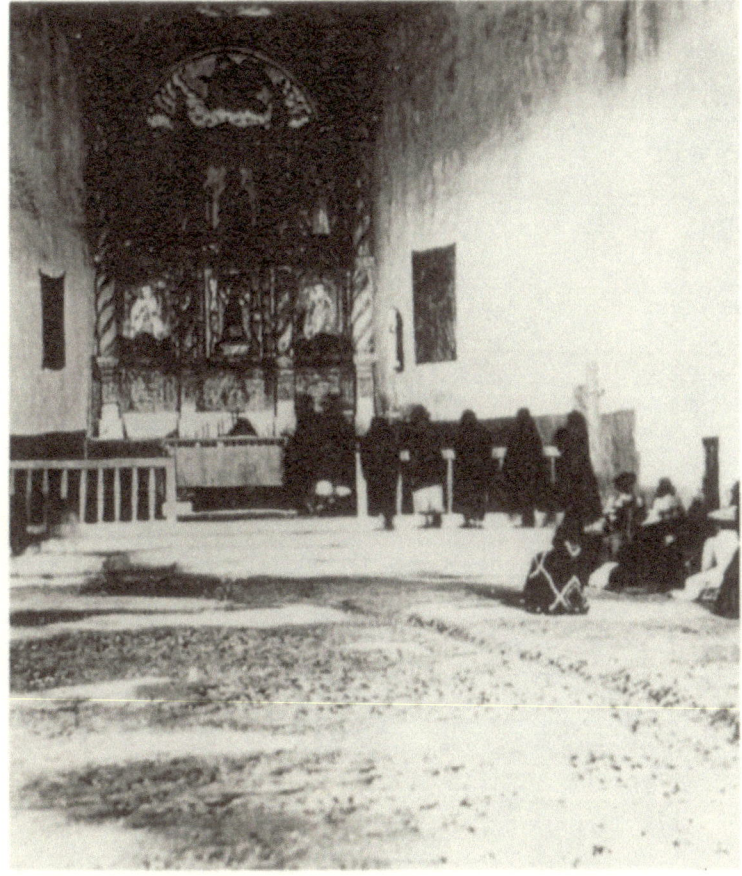

Fig. 7. Interior of the church at Acoma. Warburg's photograph.

on the priest's request, I promised him that I would attend mass the following morning.

Indians are standing before the church door (*Figure
6*). They are not easily led inside. This requires a loud call
by the chief from the three parallel village streets. At last
they assembled in the church. They are wrapped in color-
ful woolen cloths, woven in the open by nomadic Navajo
women but produced also by the Pueblos themselves.
They are ornamented in white, red, or blue and make a
most picturesque impression.

IMAGES FROM THE REGION OF THE PUEBLO INDIANS

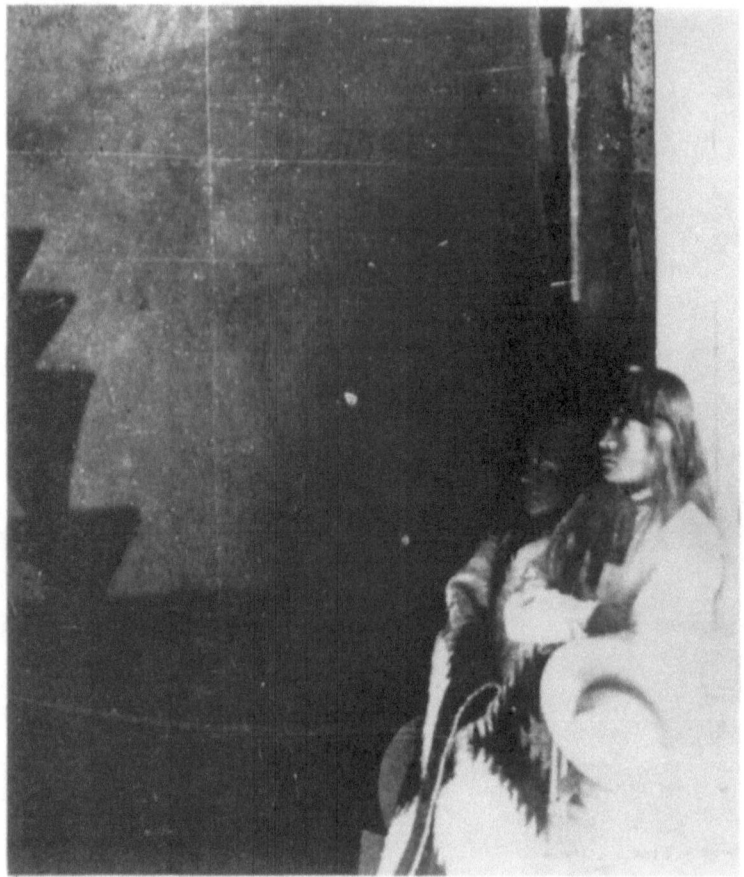

Fig. 8. Acoma. Stair-shaped roof ornamentating the church wall.
Warburg's photograph.

The interior of the church has a genuine little baroque
altar with figures of saints (*Figure 7*). The priest, who
understood not a word of the Indian language, had to
employ an interpreter who translated the mass sentence
by sentence and may well have said whatever he pleased.

It occurred to me during the service that the wall was
covered with pagan cosmologic symbols, exactly in the
style drawn for me by Cleo Jurino. The church of Laguna
is also covered with such painting, symbolizing the cos-

ABY M. WARBURG

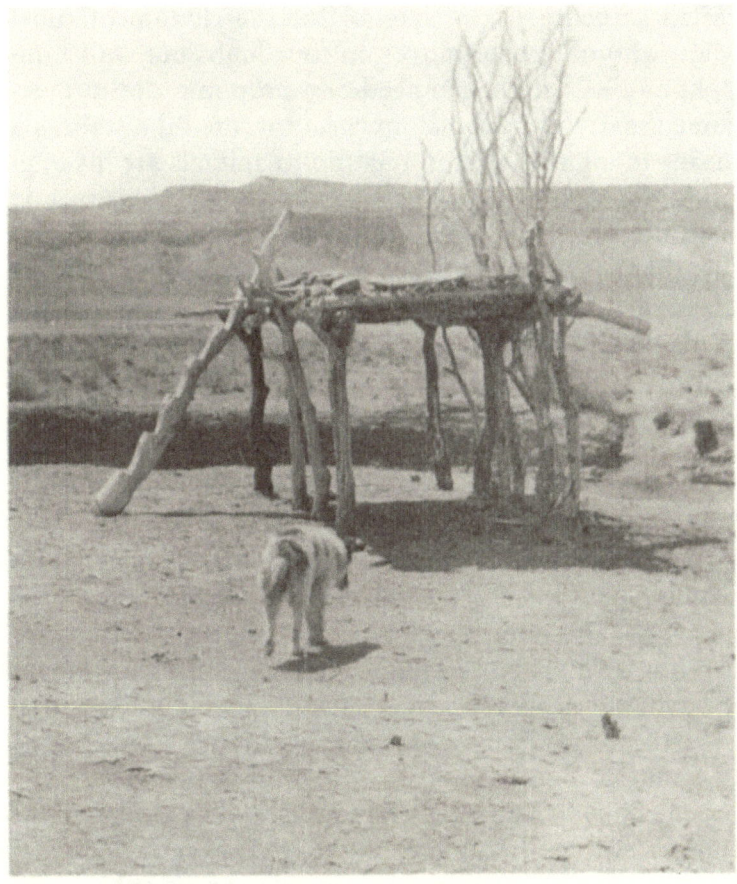

Fig. 9. Stair ornament carved from a tree. Warburg's photograph.

mos with a stair-shaped roof (*Figure 8*). The jagged ornament symbolizes a stair, and indeed not a perpendicular,
square stair but rather a much more primitive form of a
stair, carved from a tree, which still exists among the
Pueblos (*Figure 9*).

In the representation of the evolution, ascents, and
descents of nature, steps and ladders embody the primal
experiences of humanity. They are the symbol for upward
and downward struggle in space, just as the circle—the

IMAGES FROM THE REGION OF THE PUEBLO INDIANS

coiled serpent—is the symbol for the rhythm of time. Man, who no longer moves on four limbs but walks upright and is therefore in need of a prop in order to overcome gravity as he looks upward, invented the stair as a means to dignify what in relation to animals are his inferior gifts. Man, who learns to stand upright in his second year, perceives the felicity of the step because, as a creature that has to learn how to walk, he thereby receives the grace of holding his head aloft. Standing upright is the human act par excellence, the striving of the earthbound toward heaven, the uniquely symbolic act that gives to walking man the nobility of the erect and upward-turned head.

Contemplation of the sky is the grace and curse of humanity.

Thus the Indian creates the rational element in his cosmology through his equation of the worldhouse with his own staired house, which is entered by way of a ladder. But we must be careful not to regard this worldhouse as a simple expression of a spiritually tranquil cosmology; for the mistress of the worldhouse remains the uncanniest of creatures: the serpent.

The Pueblo Indian is a hunter as well as a tiller of the soil—if not to the same extent as the savage tribes that once lived in the region. He depends for his subsistence on meat as well as on corn. The masked dances, which at first seem to us like festive accessories to everyday life, are in fact magical practices for the social provision of food. The masked dance, upon which we might ordinarily look as a form of play, is in its essence an earnest, indeed warlike, measure in the fight for existence. Although the exclusion of bloody and sadistic practices makes these dances fundamentally different from the war dances of the nomadic Indians, the Pueblos' worst enemies, we must not forget that these remain, in their origin and inner tendency, dances of plunder and sacrifice. When the hunter or tiller of the soil masks himself, transforms himself into an imitation of his booty—be that animal or corn—he believes that through mysterious, mimic transformation he will be able to procure in advance what he coterminously strives to achieve through his sober, vigilant work as tiller and hunter. The dances are expressions of applied magic. The social provision of food is schizoid: magic and technology work together.

The synchrony [*Nebeneinander*] of logical civilization and fantastic, magical causation shows the Pueblo Indians' peculiar condition of hybridity and transition. They are clearly no longer primitives dependent on their senses, for whom no action directed toward the future can exist; but neither are they technologically secure Europeans, for whom future events are expected to be organically or mechanically determined. They stand on middle ground between magic and logos, and their instrument of orientation is the symbol. Between a culture of touch and a culture of thought is the culture of symbolic connection. And for this stage of symbolic thought and conduct, the dances of the Pueblo Indians are exemplary.

When I first saw the antelope dance in San Ildefonso, it struck me as quite harmless and almost comical. But for the folklorist interested in a biologic understanding of the roots of human cultural expression, there is no moment more dangerous than when he is moved to laugh at popular practices that strike him as comical. To laugh at the comical element in ethnology is wrong, because it instantly shuts off insight into the tragic element.

At San Ildefonso—a pueblo near Santa Fe which has long been under American influence—the Indians assembled for the dance. The musicians gathered first, armed with a large drum. (You can see them standing, in *Figure 10*, in front of the Mexicans on horseback.) Then the dancers arranged themselves into two parallel rows and assumed the character of the antelope in mask and posture. The two rows moved in two different ways.

IMAGES FROM THE REGION OF THE PUEBLO INDIANS

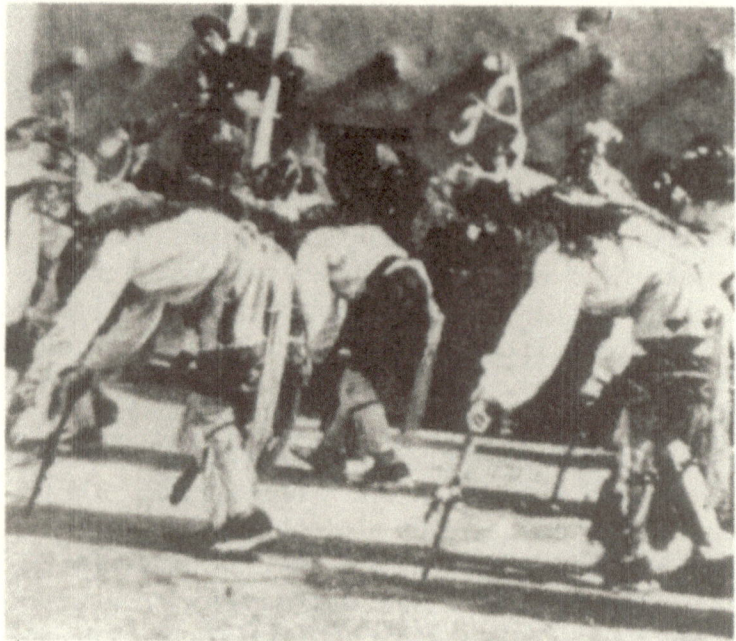

Fig. 10. Antelope dance at San Ildefonso.

Either they imitated the animal's way of walking, or
they supported themselves on their front legs—small
stilts wound with feathers—making movements with
them while standing in place. At the head of each row
stood a female figure and a hunter. With regard to the
female figure, I was able to learn only that she was
called the "mother of all animals."[3] To her the animal
mime addresses his invocations.

The insinuation into the animal mask allows the
hunting dance to simulate the actual hunt through an an-
ticipatory capture of the animal. This measure is not to
be regarded as mere play. In their bonding with the
extrapersonal, the masked dances signify for primitive
man the most thorough subordination to some alien being. When the Indian in his mimetic costume imitates, for
instance, the expressions and movements of an animal,

ABY M. WARBURG

he insinuates himself into an animal form not out of fun but, rather, to wrest something magical from nature through the transformation of his person, something he cannot attain by means of his unextended and unchanged personality.

The simulated pantomimic animal dance is thus a cultic act of the highest devotion and self-abandon to an alien being. The masked dance of so-called primitive peoples is in its original essence a document of social piety. The Indian's inner attitude to the animal is entirely different from that of the European. He regards the animal as a higher being, as the integrity of its animal nature makes it a much more gifted creature than man, its weaker counterpart.

My initiation into the psychology of the will to animal metamorphosis came, just before my departure, from Frank Hamilton Cushing, the pioneering and veteran explorer of the Indian psyche. I found his insights personally overwhelming. This pockmarked man with sparse reddish hair and of inscrutable age, smoking a cigarette, said to me that an Indian had once told him, why should man stand taller than animals? "Take a good look at the antelope, she is all running, and runs so much better than man—or the bear, who is all strength. Men can only *do* in part what the animal *is,* totally." This fairy-tale way of thinking, no matter how odd it may sound, is the preliminary to our scientific, genetic explanation of the world. These Indian pagans, like pagans all over the world, form an attachment out of reverential awe—what is known as totemism—to the animal world, by believing in animals of all kinds as the mythical ancestors of their tribes. Their explanation of the world as inorganically coherent is not so far removed from Darwinism; for whereas we impute natural law to the autonomous process of evolution in nature, the pagans attempt to explain it through arbitrary identification with the animal world. It is, one might say, a Darwinism of mythical elective affinity which determines the lives of these so-called primitive people.

The formal survival of the hunting dance in San Ildefonso is obvious. But when we consider that the antelope has been extinct there for more than three generations, then it may well be that we have in the antelope dance a transition to the purely demoniac kachina dances, the chief task of which is to pray for a good crop harvest. In Oraibi, for example, there exists still today an antelope clan, whose chief task is weather magic.

Whereas the imitative animal dance must be understood in terms of the mimic magic of hunting culture, the kachina dances, corresponding to cyclic peasant festivals, have a character entirely of their own which, however, is revealed only at sites far removed from European culture. This cultic, magical masked dance, with its entreaties focused on inanimate nature, can be observed in its more or less original form only where the railroads have yet to penetrate and where—as in the Moki villages—even the veneer of offical Catholicism no longer exists.

The children are taught to regard the kachinas with a deep religious awe. Every child takes the kachinas for supernatural, terrifying creatures, and the moment of the child's initiation into the nature of the kachinas, into the society of masked dancers itself, represents the most important turning point in the education of the Indian child.

On the market square of the rock village of Oraibi, the most remote westerly point, I was lucky enough to observe a so-called humiskachina dance. Here I saw the living originals of the masked dancers I had already seen in puppet form in a room of this same village of Oraibi.

To reach Oraibi, I had to travel for two days from the railway station of Holbrook in a small carriage. This is a so-called buggy with four light wheels, capable of advancing through desert sands where only gorse can grow. The driver throughout my stay in the region was Frank

ABY M. WARBURG

Allen, a Mormon. We experienced a very strong sand-storm, which completely obliterated the wagon tracks—the only navigational aid in this roadless steppe. We had the good luck nevertheless to arrive after our two days' journey in Keams Canyon, where we were greeted by Mr. Keam, a most hospitable Irishman.

From this spot I was able to make the actual excursions to the cliff villages, which extend from north to south on three parallel rock formations. I arrived first at the remarkable village of Walpi. It is romantically perched on the rock crest, its stair-shaped houses rising in stone masses like towers from the rock. A narrow path on the high rock leads past the masses of houses. The illustration shows the desolation and severity of this rock and its houses, as they project themselves into the world (*Figures 11 and 12*).

Very similar in its overall impression to Walpi is Oraibi, where I was able to observe the humiskachina dance. Up on top, on the marketplace of the cliff village, where an old blind man sits with his goat, a dancing area was being prepared (*Figure 13*). This humiskachina dance is the dance of the growing corn. On the evening before the actual dance, I was inside the kiva, where secret ceremonies take place. It contained no fetish altar. The Indians simply sat and smoked ceremonially. Every now and then a pair of brown legs descended from above on the ladder, followed by the whole man attached to them.

The young men were busy painting their masks for the following day. They use their big leather helmets again and again, as new ones would be too costly. The painting process involves taking water into the mouth and then spraying it onto the leather mask as the colors are rubbed in.

By the following morning, the entire audience, including two groups of children, had assembled on the wall (*Figure 14*). The Indians' relationship to their chil-

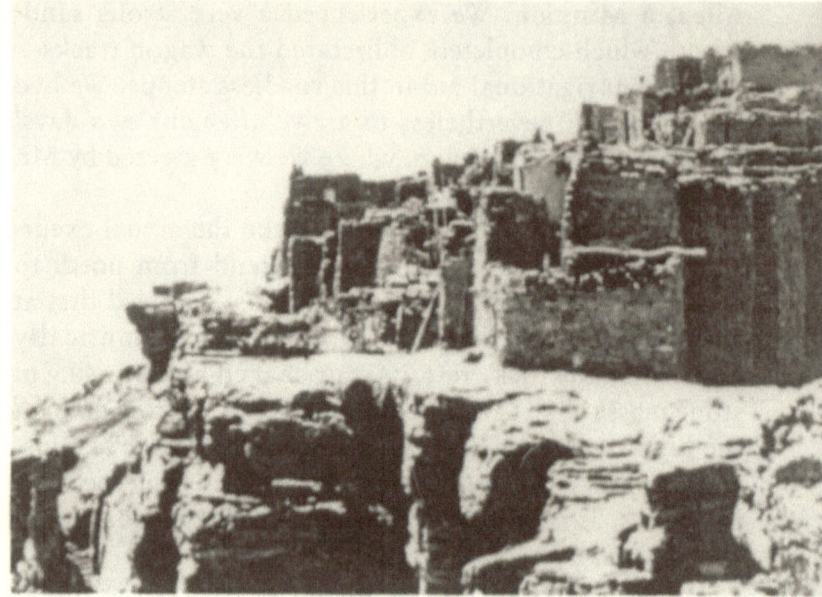

Fig. 11. Walpi. Warburg's photograph.

Fig. 12. Walpi. Warburg's photograph.

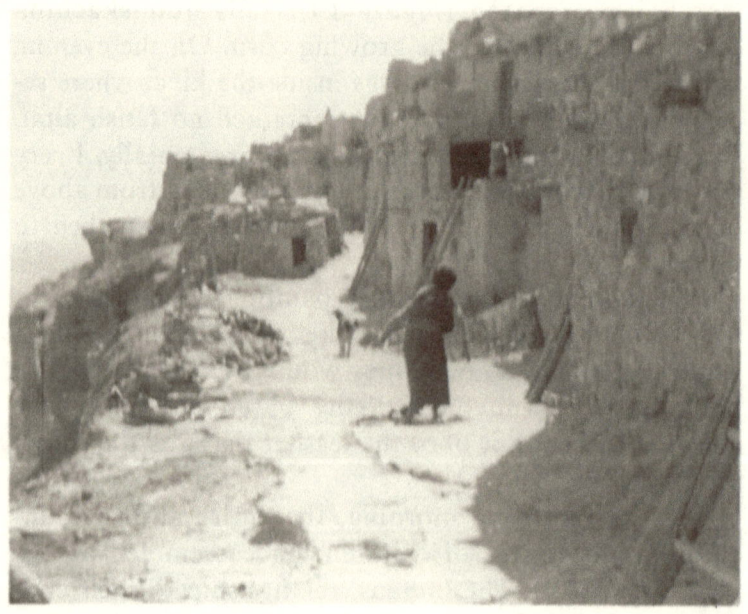

ABY M. WARBURG

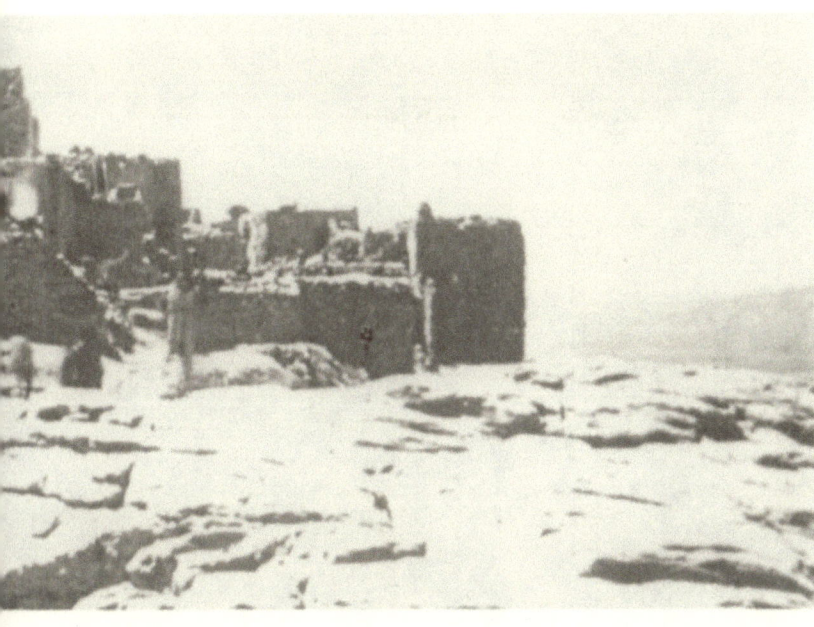

Fig. 13. Blind man at dancing area, Oraibi. Warburg's photograph.

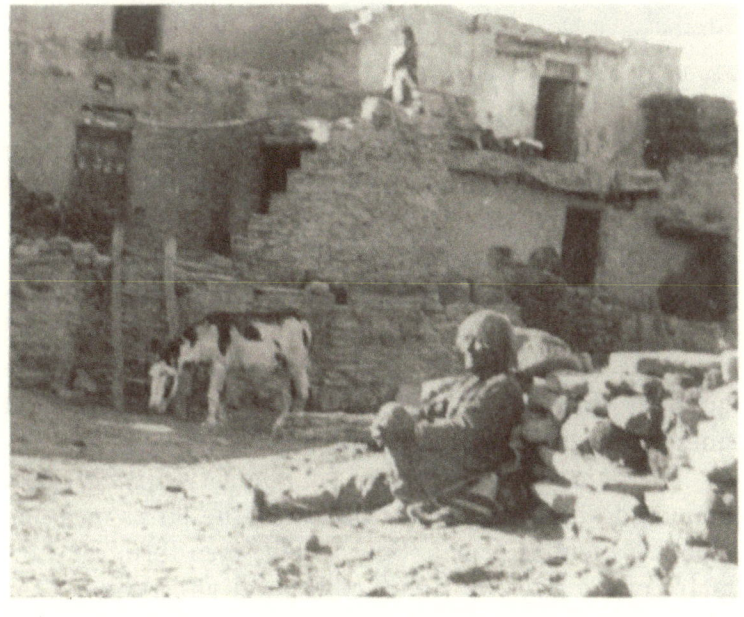

IMAGES FROM THE REGION OF THE PUEBLO INDIANS

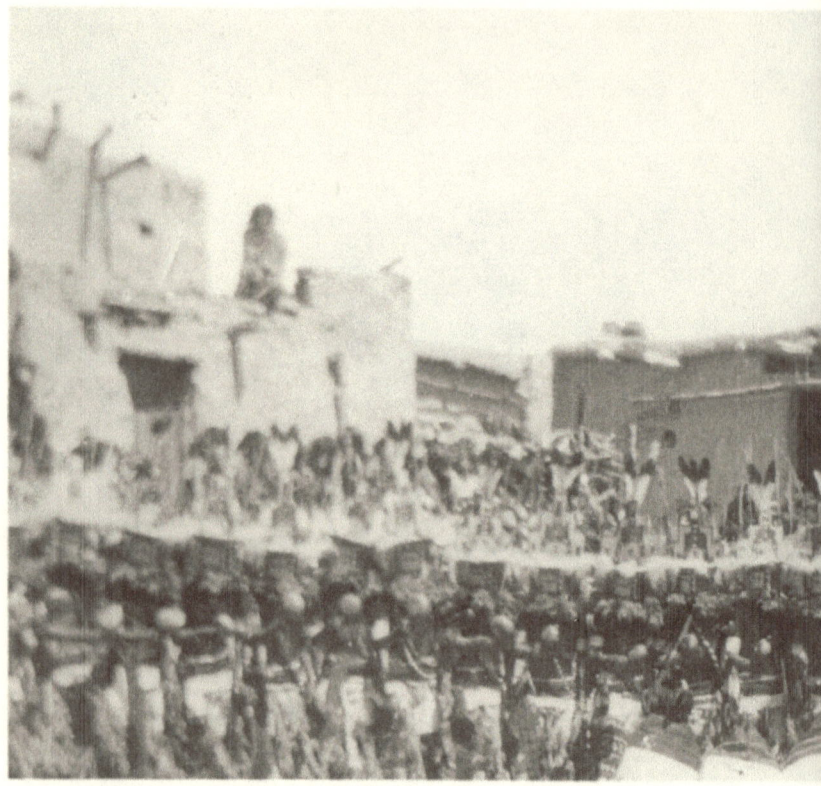

Fig. 14. Humiskachina dancers, Oraibi.

dren is extraordinarily appealing. Children are brought up gently but with discipline and are very obliging, once one has earned their trust. Now the children had assembled, with earnest anticipation, on the marketplace. These humiskachina figures with artificial heads move them to real terror, all the more so as they have learned from the kachina dolls of the inflexible and fearsome qualities of the masks. Who knows whether our dolls did not also originate as such demons?

The dance was performed by about twenty-to-thirty male and about ten female dancers—the latter meaning men representing female figures. Five men form the vanguard of the two-row dance configuration. Although the

ABY M. WARBURG

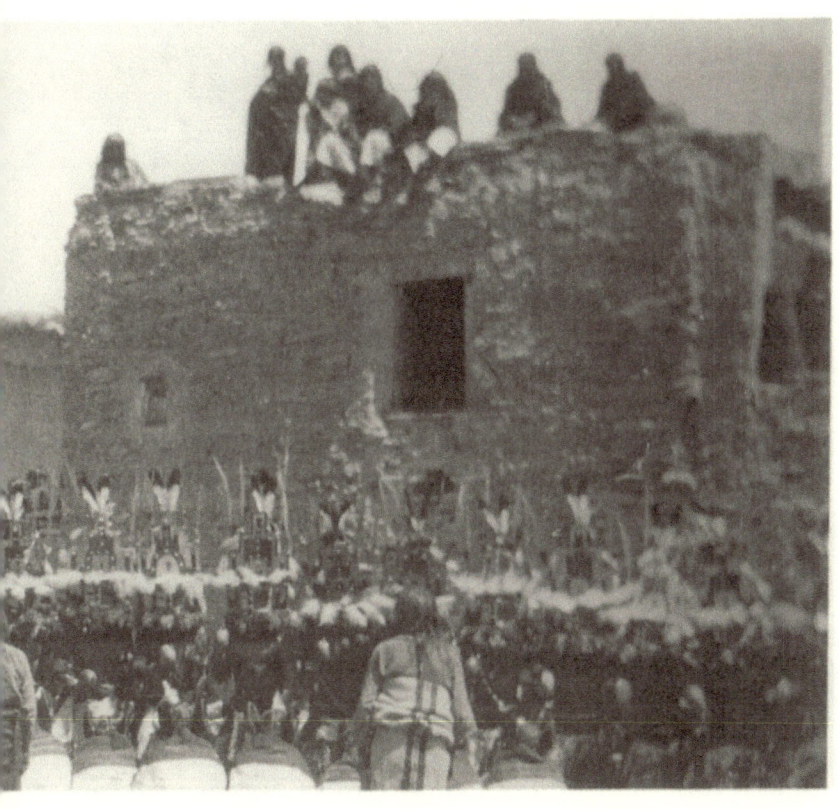

dance is performed on the market square, the dancers have an architectonic focus, and that is the stone structure in which a small dwarf pine has been placed, adorned with feathers. This is a small temple where the prayers and chants accompanying the masked dances are offered. Devotion flows from this little temple in the most striking manner.

The dancers' masks are green and red, traversed diagonally by a white stripe punctuated by three dots (*Figures 15 and 16*). These, I was told, are raindrops, and the symbolic representations on the helmet also show the stair-shaped cosmos with the source of rain identified again by semicircular clouds and short strokes emanating

IMAGES FROM THE REGION OF THE PUEBLO INDIANS

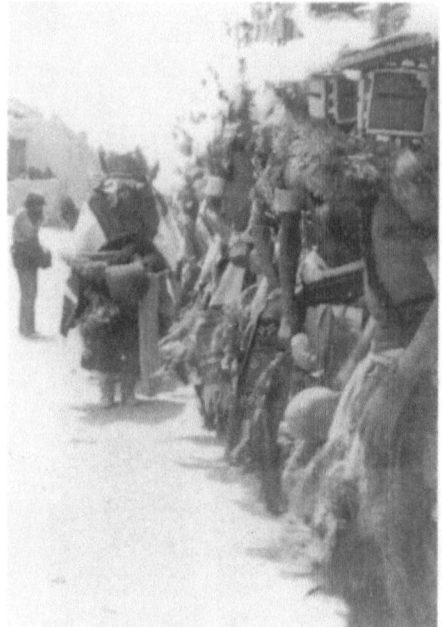
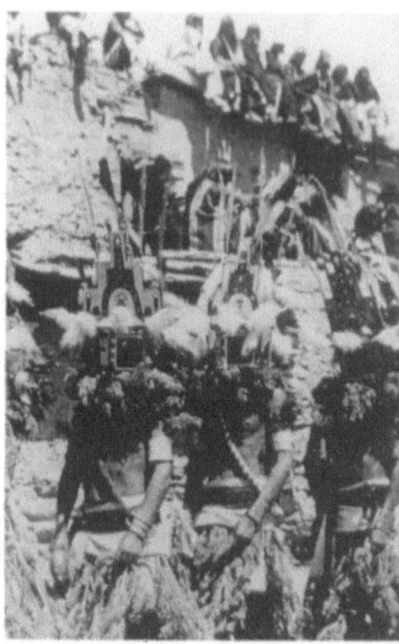

Fig. 15. Humiskachina dancers, Oraibi.   Fig. 16. Humiskachina dancers, Oraibi.

from them. These symbols appear as well on the woven wraps the dancers wind around their bodies: red and green ornaments gracefully woven on a white background (*Figure 17*). In one hand, each male dancer holds a rattle carved from a hollow gourd and filled with stones. And at each knee he wears a tortoise shell hung with pebbles, so that the rattle noises issue from the knees as well (*Figure 18*).

The chorus performs two different acts. Either the girls sit in front of the men and make music with a rattle and a piece of wood, while the men's dance configuration consists of one after another turning, in solitary rotation; or, alternately, the women rise and accompany the rotating movements of the men. Throughout the dance, two priests sprinkle consecrated flour on the dancers (*Figure 19*).

The women's dance costume consists of a cloth cover-

ABY M. WARBURG

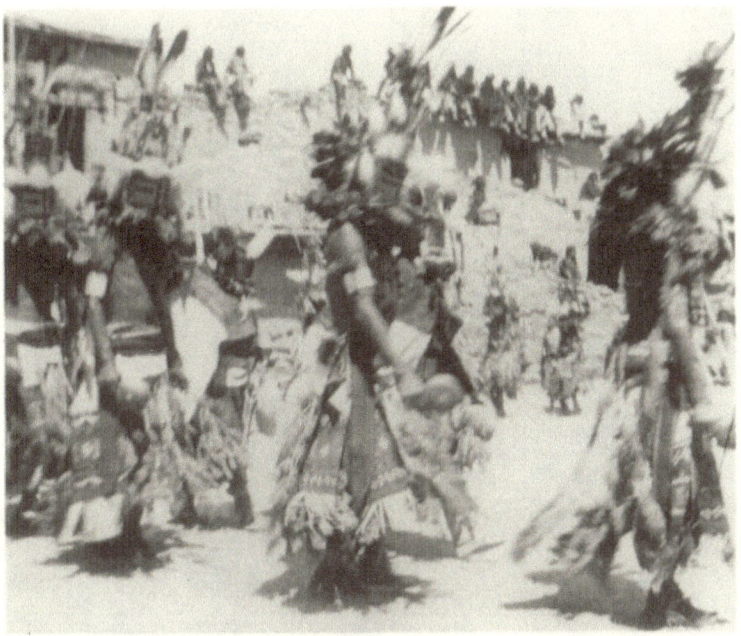

Fig. 17. Humiskachina dancers, Oraibi.

ing the entire body, so as not to show that these are, in fact, men. The mask is adorned, on either side at the top, with the curious anemonelike hairdo that is the specific hair adornment of the Pueblo girls (*Figures 20 and 21*). Red-dyed horsehair hanging from the masks symbolizes rain, and rain ornamentation appears as well on the shawls and other wrappings.

During the dance, the dancers are sprinkled by a priest with holy flour, and all the while the dance configuration remains connected at the head of the line to the little temple. The dance lasts from morning till evening. In the intervals the Indians leave the village and go to a

Fig. 18. Overleaf:
Humiskachina dancers, Oraibi.

IMAGES FROM THE REGION OF THE PUEBLO INDIANS

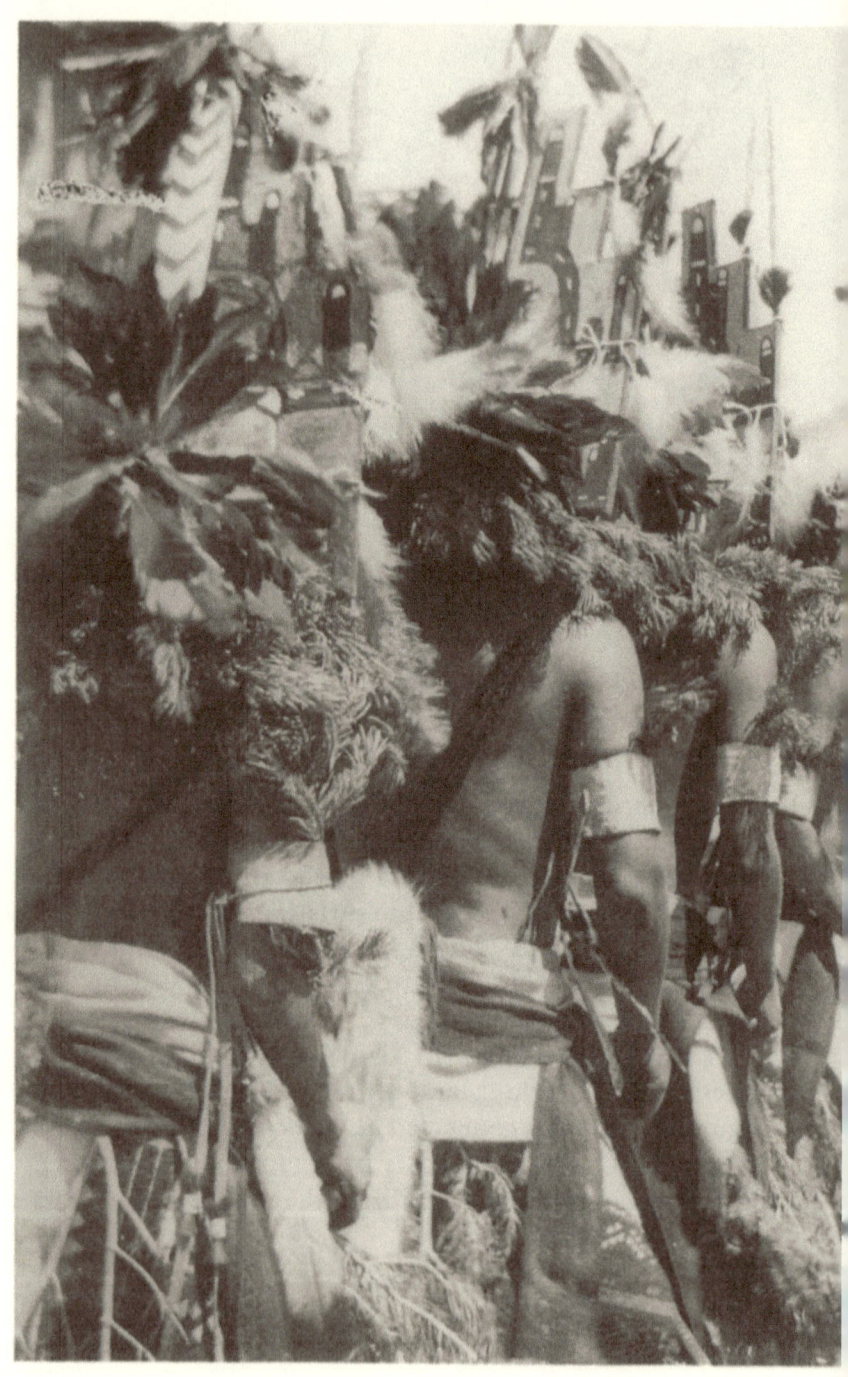

ABY M. WARBURG

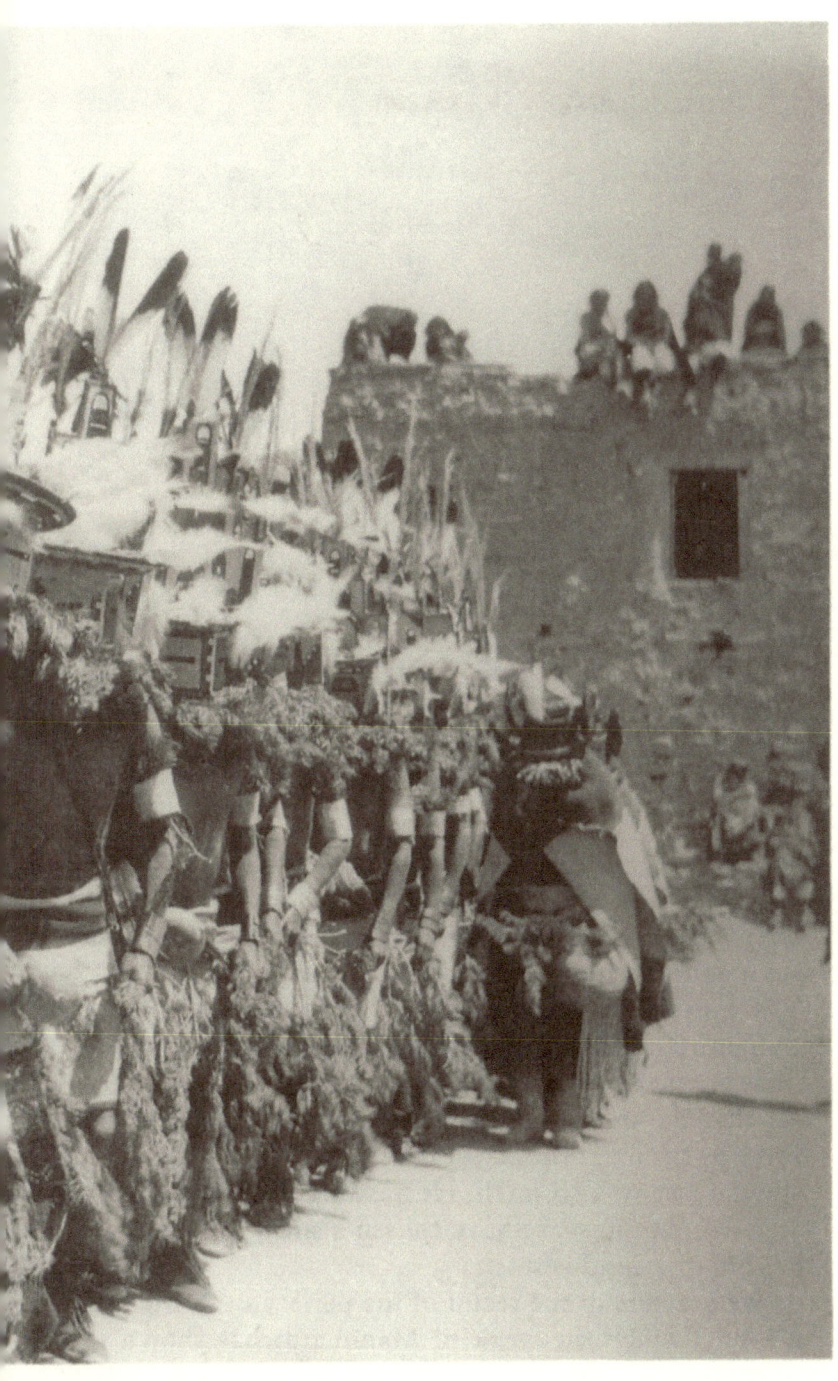

IMAGES FROM THE REGION OF THE PUEBLO INDIANS

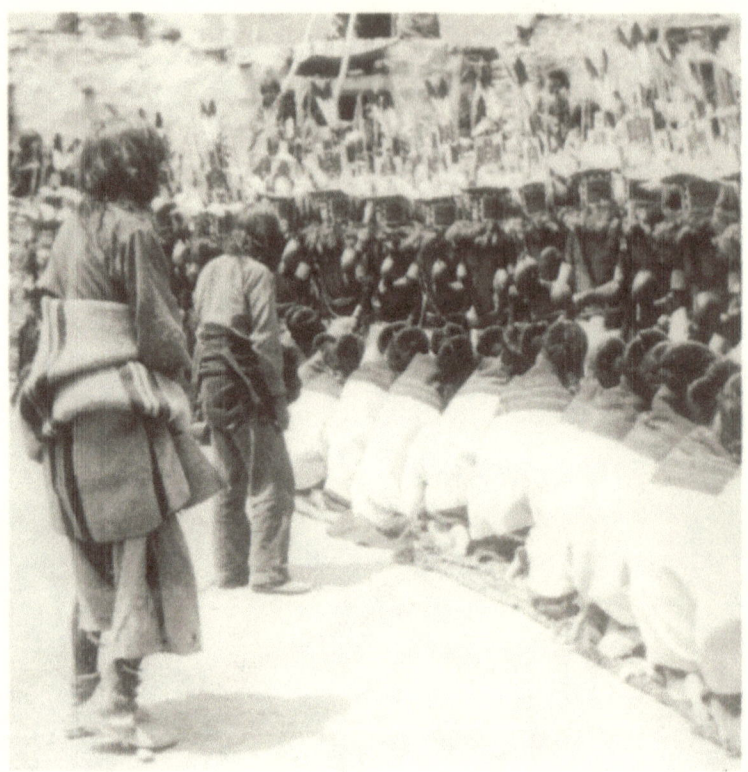

Fig. 19. Humiskachina dancers, Oraibi.

rocky ledge to rest for a moment (*Figure 22*). Whoever
sees a dancer without his mask, will die.

The little temple is the actual focal point of the dance
configuration. It is a little tree, adorned with feathers.
These are the so-called Nakwakwocis. I was struck by the
fact that the tree was so small. I went to the old chief,
who was sitting at the edge of the square, and asked him
why the tree was so small. He answered: we once had a
large tree, but now we have chosen a small one, because
the soul of a child is small.

We are here in the realm of the perfect animistic and
tree cult, which the work of Mannhardt has shown to

ABY M. WARBURG

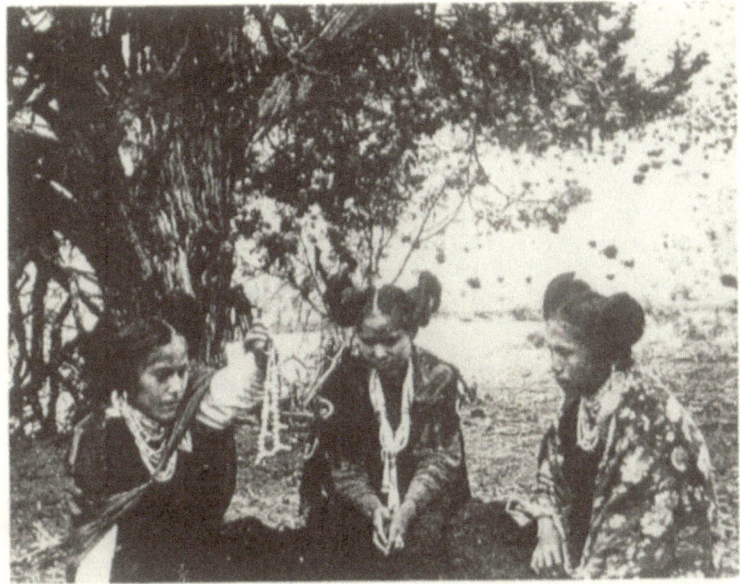

Fig. 20. "Anemone" hairdos.

Fig. 21. "Anemone" hairdos.

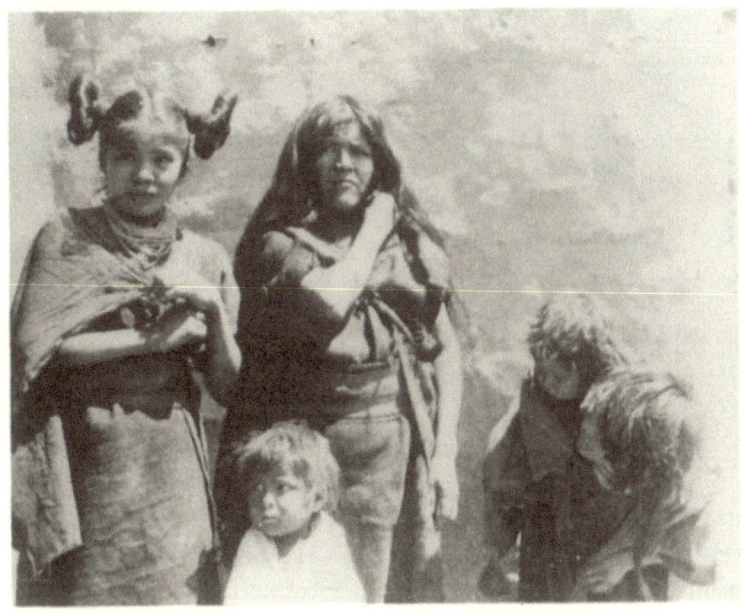

IMAGES FROM THE REGION OF THE PUEBLO INDIANS

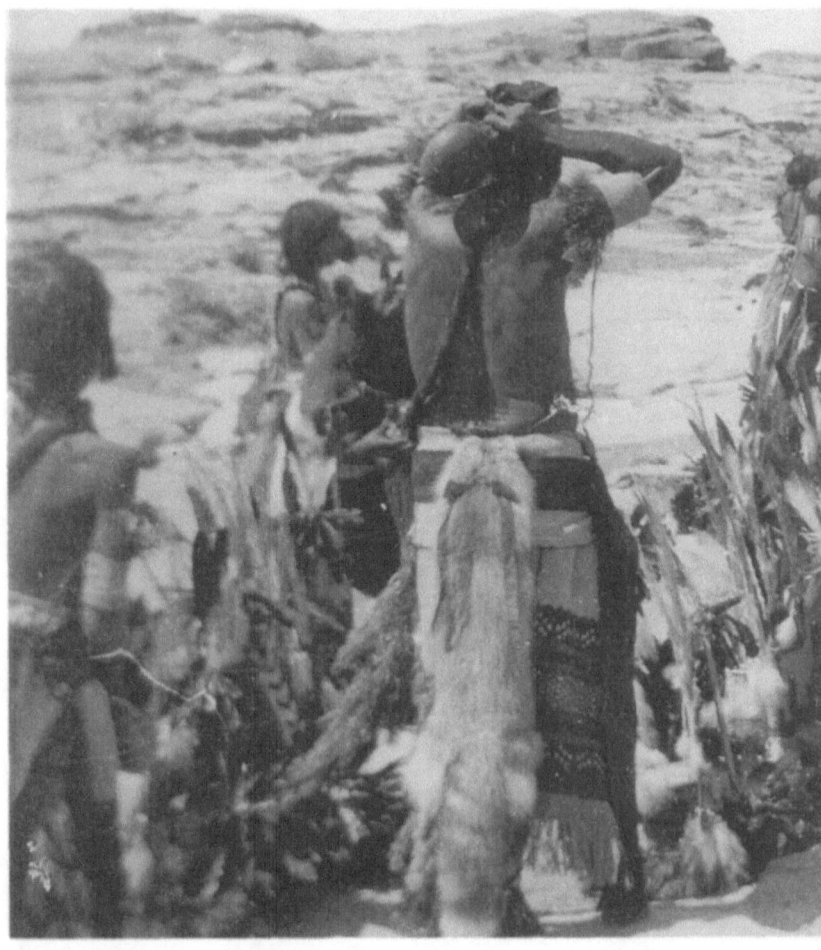

Fig. 22. Dancers at rest, Oraibi.

belong to the universal religious patrimony of primitive
peoples, and it has survived from European paganism
down to the harvest customs of the present day. It is here
a question of establishing a bond between natural forces
and man, of creating a symbol as the connecting agent,
indeed as the magical rite that achieves integration by
sending out a mediator, in this case a tree, more closely
bound to the earth than man, because it grows from the

ABY M. WARBURG

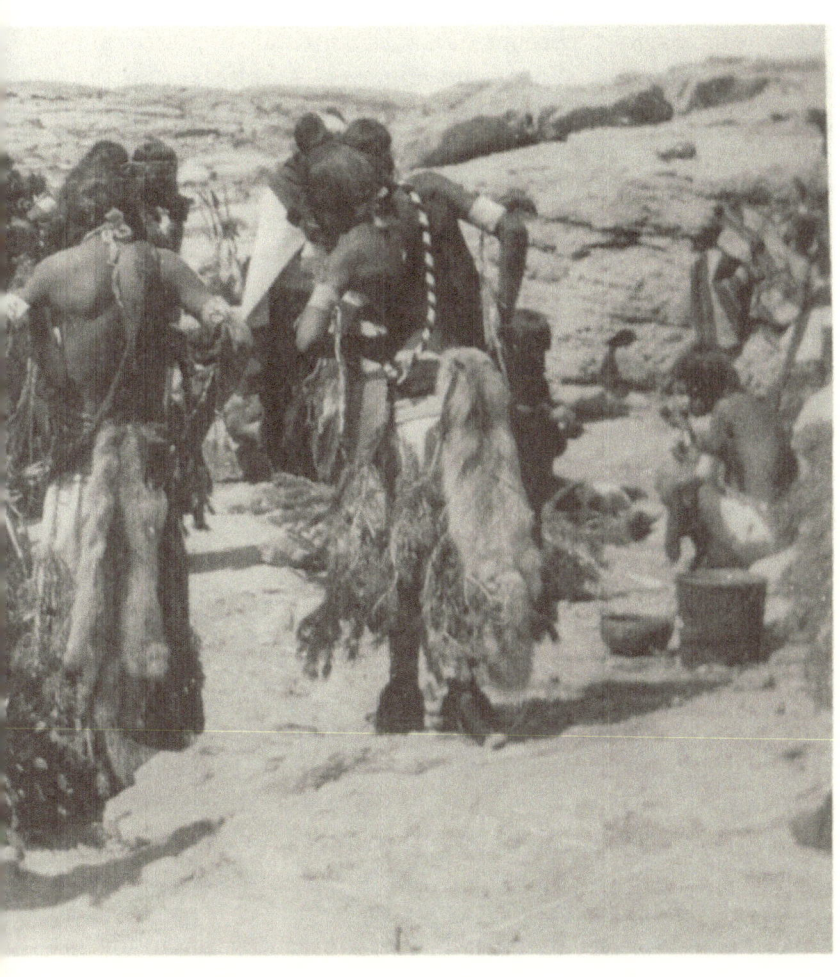

earth. This tree is the nature-given mediator, opening the
way to the subterranean element.

The next day the feathers are carried down to a certain spring in the valley and either planted there or else
hung as votive offerings. These are to put into effect the
prayer for fertilization, resulting in a plentiful and
healthy crop of corn.

Late in the afternoon the dancers resume their inde-

IMAGES FROM THE REGION OF THE PUEBLO INDIANS

fatigable, earnest ceremonial and continue to perform their unchanging dance movements. As the sun was about to sink, we were presented with an astonishing spectacle, one which showed with overwhelming clarity how solemn and silent composure draws its magical religious forms from the very depths of elemental humanity. In this light, our tendency to view the spiritual element alone in such ceremonies must be rejected as a one-sided and paltry mode of explanation.

Six figures appeared. Three almost completely naked men smeared with yellow clay, their hair wound into horn shapes, were dressed only in loin cloths. Then came three men in women's clothes. And while the chorus and its priests proceeded with their dance movements, undisturbed and with unbroken devotion, these figures launched into a thoroughly vulgar and disrespectful parody of the chorus movements. And no one laughed. The vulgar parody was regarded not as comic mockery but, rather, as a kind of peripheral contribution by the revellers, in the effort to ensure a fruitful corn year. Anyone familiar with ancient tragedy will see here the duality of tragic chorus and satyr play, "grafted onto a single stem." The ebb and flow of nature appears in anthropomorphic symbols: not in a drawing but in the dramatic magical dance, actually returned to life.

The essence of magical insinuation into the divine, into a share of its superhuman power, is revealed in the terrifyingly dramatic aspect of Mexican religious devotion. In one festival a woman is worshipped for forty days as a corn goddess and then sacrificed, and then the priest slips into the skin of the poor creature. Compared to this most elementary and frenzied attempt to approach the divinity, what we observed among the Pueblos is indeed related but infinitely more refined. Yet there is no guarantee that the sap does not still rise in secret from such blood-soaked cultic roots. After all, the same soil that bears the Pueblos has also witnessed the war dances

ABY M. WARBURG

of the wild, nomadic Indians, with their atrocities culminating in the martyrdom of the enemy.

The most extreme approximation of this magical desire for unity with nature via the animal world can be observed among the Moki Indians, in their dance with live serpents at Oraibi and Walpi. I did not myself observe this dance, but a few photographs will give an idea of this most pagan of all the ceremonies of Walpi. This dance is at once an animal dance and a religious, seasonal dance. In it, the individual animal dance of San Ildefonso and the individual fertility ritual of the Oraibi humiskachina dance converge in an intense expressive effort. For in August, when the critical moment in the tilling of the soil arrives to render the entire crop harvest contingent on rainstorms, these redemptive storms are invoked through a dance with live serpents, celebrated alternately in Oraibi and Walpi. Whereas in San Ildefonso only a simulated version of antelope is visible—at least to the uninitiated—and the corn dance achieves the demoniac representation of corn demons only with masks, we find here in Walpi a far more primeval aspect of the magic dance.

Here the dancers and the live animal form a magical unity, and the surprising thing is that the Indians have found in these dance ceremonies a way of handling the most dangerous of all animals, the rattlesnake, so that it can be tamed without violence, so that the creature will participate willingly—or at least without making use of its aggressive abilities, unless provoked—in ceremonies lasting for days. This would surely lead to catastrophe in the hands of Europeans.

Two Moki clans provide the participants in the serpent ceremony: the antelope and the serpent clans, both of whom are folklorically and totemistically linked with the two animals. That totemism can be taken seriously even today is proved here, as humans not only appear masked as animals but enter into cultic exchange with the most dangerous beast, the live serpent. The serpent ceremony at Walpi thus stands between simulated, mimic empathy and bloody sacrifice. It involves not the imitation of the animal but the bluntest engagement with it as a ritual participant—and that not as sacrifical victim but, like the *baho,* as fellow rainmaker.

For the snakes themselves, the serpent dance at Walpi is an enforced entreaty. They are caught live in the desert in August, when the storms are imminent, and in a sixteen-day ceremony in Walpi they are attended to in the underground kiva by the chiefs of the serpent and antelope clans in a series of unique ceremonies, of which the most significant and the most astonishing for white observers is the washing of the snakes. The snake is treated like a novice of the mysteries, and notwithstanding its resistance, its head is dipped in consecrated, medicated water. Then it is thrown onto a sand painting done on the kiva floor and representing four lightning snakes with a quadruped in the middle. In another kiva a sand painting depicts a mass of clouds from which emerge four differently colored lightning streaks, corresponding to the points of the compass, in the form of serpents. Onto the first sand painting, each snake is hurled with great force, so that the drawing is obliterated and the serpent is absorbed into the sand. I am convinced that this magic throw is intended to force the serpent to invoke lightning or produce rain. That is clearly the significance of the entire ceremony, and the ceremonies that follow prove that these consecrated serpents join the Indians in the starkest manner as provokers and petitioners of rain. They are living rain serpent–saints in animal form.

The serpents—numbering about a hundred and including a distinct number of genuine rattlesnakes with, as has been ascertained, their poisonous fangs left intact— are guarded in the kiva, and on the festival's final day they are imprisoned in a bush with a band wound around it. The ceremony culminates as follows: approach to the

ABY M. WARBURG

bush, seizing and carrying of the live serpents, dispatching of the snakes to the plains as messengers. American researchers describe the clutching of the snake as an unbelievably exciting act. It is carried out in the following way.

A group of three approaches the serpent bush. The high priest of the serpent clan pulls a snake from the bush as another Indian with painted face and tattoos, wearing a fox skin on his back, clutches the snake and places it in his mouth. A companion, holding him by the shoulders, distracts the attention of the serpent by waving a feathered stick. The third figure is the guard and the snake catcher, in case the serpent should slip out of the second man's mouth. The dance is played out in just over half an hour on the small square at Walpi. When all the snakes have thus been carried for a while to the sound of rattles—produced by the Indians who wear rattles and stone-filled tortoise shells on their knees—they are borne by the dancers with lightning speed into the plain, where they disappear.

From what we know of Walpi mythology, this form of devotion certainly goes back to ancestral, cosmologic legend. One saga tells the story of the hero Ti-yo, who undertakes a subterranean journey to discover the source of the longed-for water. He passes the various kivas of the princes of the underworld, always accompanied by a female spider who sits invisibly on his right ear—an Indian Virgil, Dante's guide to the underworld—and eventually guides him past the two sun houses of the West and East into the great serpent kiva, where he receives the magic *baho* that will invoke the weather. According to the saga, Ti-yo returns from the underworld with the *baho* and two serpent-maidens, who bear him serpentine children—very dangerous creatures who ultimately force the tribes to change their dwelling place. The serpents are woven into this myth both as weather deities and as totems that bring about the migration of the clans.

IMAGES FROM THE REGION OF THE PUEBLO INDIANS

In this snake dance the serpent is therefore not sacrificed but rather, through consecration and suggestive dance mimicry, transformed into a messenger and dispatched, so that, returned to the souls of the dead, it may in the form of lightning produce storms from the heavens. We have here an insight into the pervasiveness of myth and magical practice among primitive humanity.

The elementary form of emotional release through Indian magical practice may strike the layman as a characteristic unique to primitive wildness, of which Europe knows nothing. And yet two thousand years ago in the very cradle of our own European culture, in Greece, cultic habits were in vogue which in crudeness and perversity far surpass what we have seen among the Indians.

In the orgiastic cult of Dionysus, for example, the Maenads danced with snakes in one hand and wore live serpents as diadems in their hair, holding in the other hand the animal that was to be ripped to pieces in the ascetic sacrificial dance in honor of the god. In contrast to the dance of the Moki Indians of today, blood sacrifice in a state of frenzy is the culmination and fundamental significance of this religious dance (*Figure 23*).

The deliverance from blood sacrifice as the innermost ideal of purification pervades the history of religious evolution from east to west. The serpent shares in this process of religious sublimation. Its role can be considered a yardstick for the changing nature of faith from fetishism to the pure religion of redemption. In the Old Testament, as in the case of the primal serpent Tiamat in Babylon, the serpent is the spirit of evil and of temptation. In Greece, as well, it is the merciless, devouring creature of the underworld: the Erinyes are encircled by snakes, and when the gods mete out punishment they send a serpent as their executioner.

This idea of the serpent as a destroying force from the underworld has found its most powerful and tragic sym-

ABY M. WARBURG

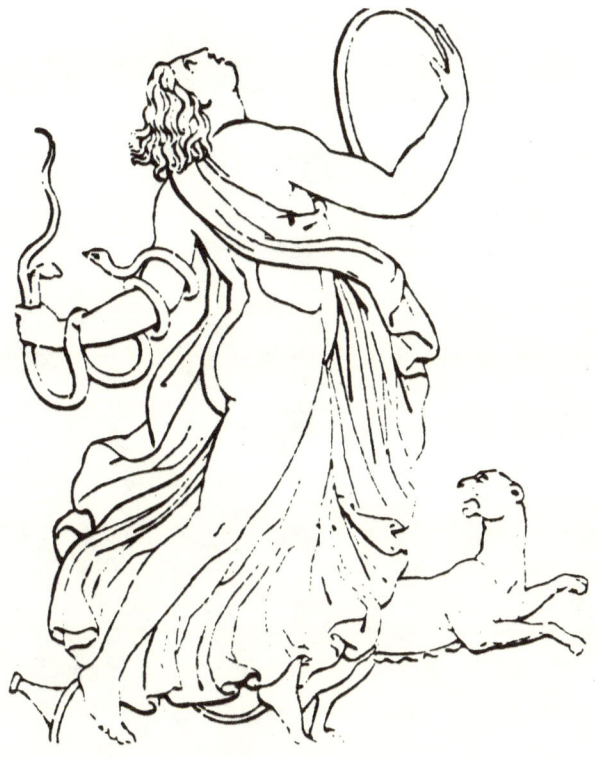

Fig. 23. Dancing Maenad. Musée du Louvre, Paris.

bol in the myth and in the sculpted group of Laocoon. The vengeance of the gods, wrought on their priest and on his two sons by means of a strangler serpent, becomes in this renowned sculpture of antiquity the manifest incarnation of extreme human suffering. The soothsaying priest who wanted to come to the aid of his people by warning them of the wiles of the Greeks falls victim to the revenge of the partial gods. Thus the death of the father and his sons becomes a symbol of ancient suffering: death at the hands of vengeful demons, without justice and without hope of redemption. That is the hopeless, tragic pessimism of antiquity (*Figure 24*).

The serpent as the demon in the pessimistic world

IMAGES FROM THE REGION OF THE PUEBLO INDIANS

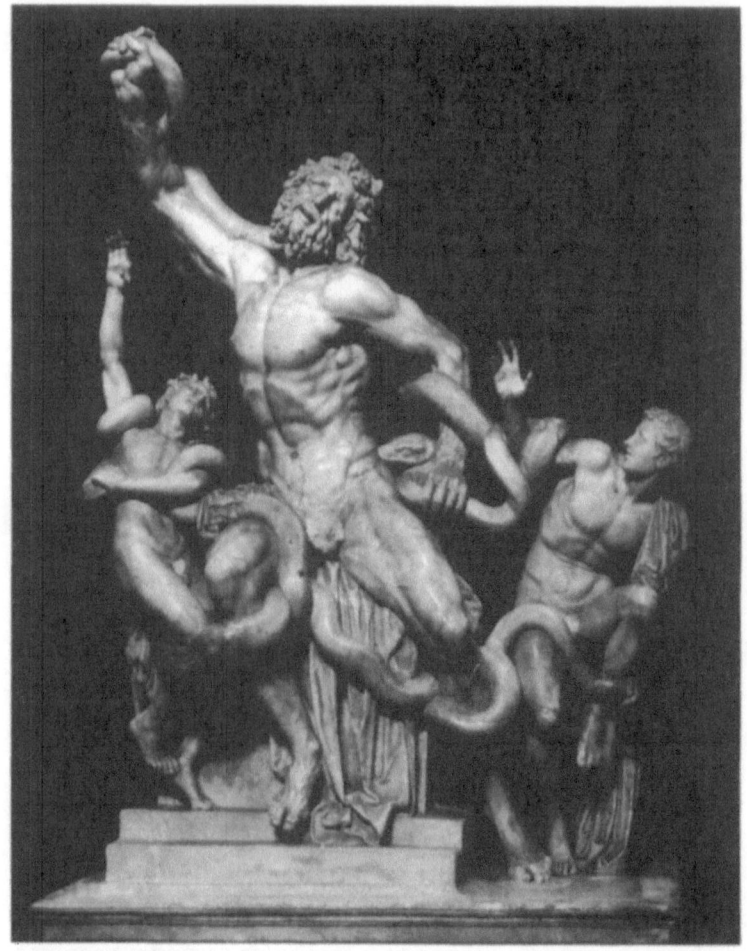

Fig. 24. Laocoon group. Vatican Museum, Rome. Alinari/Art Resource, N. Y.

Fig. 25. Facing: Asclepius. Musei Capitolini, Rome.

ABY M. WARBURG

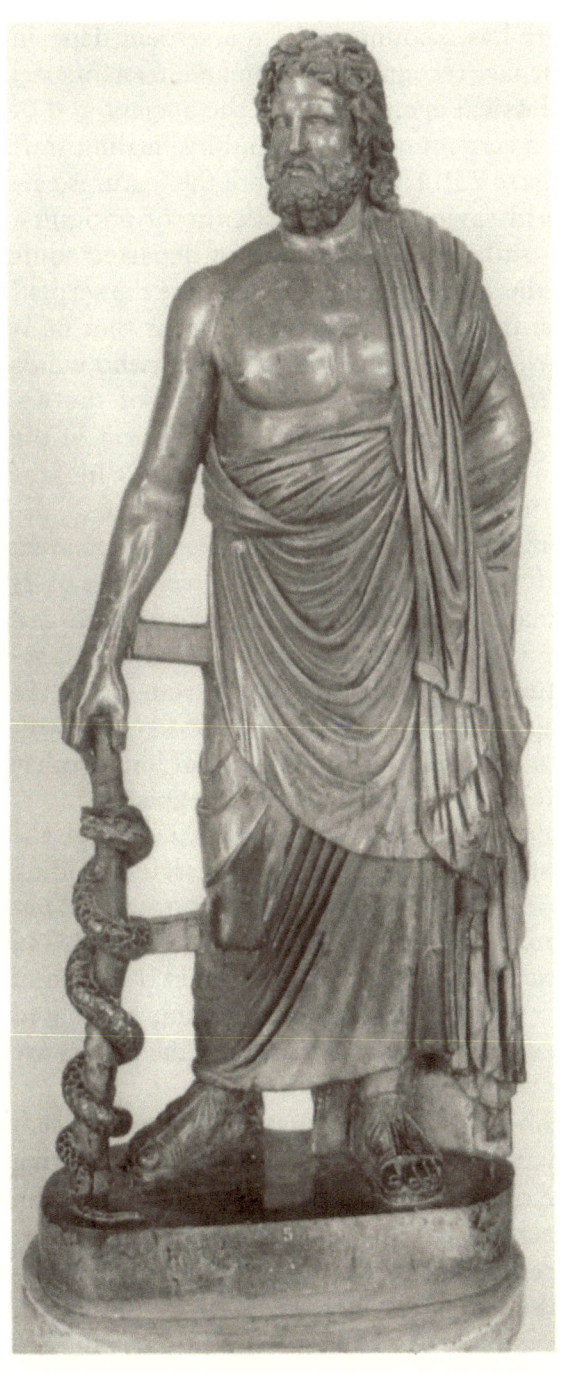

IMAGES FROM THE REGION OF THE PUEBLO INDIANS

view of antiquity has a counterpart in a serpent-deity in which we can at last recognize the humane, transfigured beauty of the classical age. Asclepius, the ancient god of healing, carries a serpent coiling around his healing staff as a symbol (*Figure 25*). His features are the features carried by the world savior in the plastic art of antiquity. And this most exalted and serene god of departed souls has his roots in the subterranean realm, where the serpent makes its home. It is in the form of a serpent that he is accorded his earliest devotion. It is he himself who winds around his staff: namely, the departed soul of the deceased, which survives and reappears in the form of the serpent. For the snake is not only, as Cushing's Indians would say, the fatal bite in readiness or fulfillment, destroying without mercy; the snake also reveals by its own ability to cast off its slough, slipping, as it were, out of its own mortal remains, how a body can leave its skin and yet continue to live. It can slither into the earth and re-emerge. The return from within the earth, from where the dead rest, along with the capacity for bodily renewal, makes the snake the most natural symbol of immortality and of rebirth from sickness and mortal anguish.[4]

In the temple of Asclepius at Kos in Asia Minor the god stood transfigured in human form, a statue holding in his hand the staff with the serpent coiled around it. But his truest and most powerful essence was not revealed in this lifeless mask of stone but lived instead in the form of a serpent in the temple's innermost sanctum: fed, cared for, and attended in cultic devotion as only the Mokis are able to care for their serpents.

On a Spanish calendar leaf from the thirteenth century, which I found in a Vatican manuscript, representing Asclepius as the ruler of the month in the sign of Scorpio, significant aspects of the Asclepian serpent cult are revealed in their coarseness as well as their refinement (*Figure 26*). We can see here, hieroglyphically indicated, ritual acts from the cult of Kos in thirty sections, all iden-

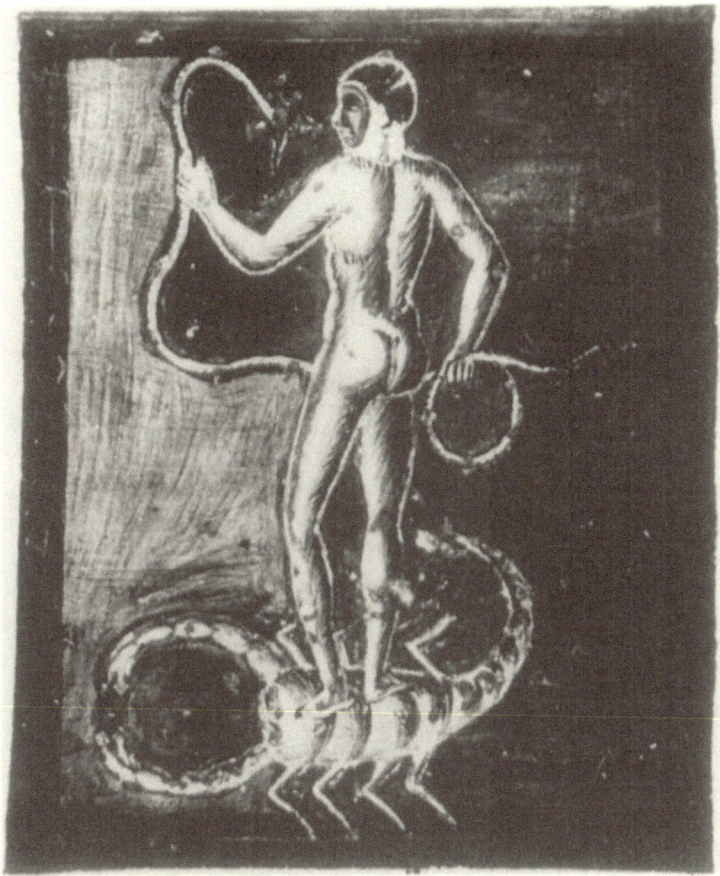

Fig. 26. Asclepius with serpent on the sign of the Scorpion. MS Vossianus Leyden. Voss. Lat. Q 79.

tical to the crude, magical desire of the Indians to enter the realm of the serpent. We see the rite of incubation and the serpent as it is carried by human hands and worshipped as a deity of the springs.

This medieval manuscript is astrological. In other words, it shows these ritual forms not as prescriptions for devotional practices, as had previously been the case; rather, these figures have become hieroglyphs for those

IMAGES FROM THE REGION OF THE PUEBLO INDIANS

born under the heavenly sign of Asclepius. For Asclepius has become precisely a star-deity, undergoing a transformation through an act of cosmologic imagination which has completely deprived him of the real, the direct susceptibility to influence, the subterranean, the lowly. As a fixed star he stands over Scorpio in the zodiac. He is surrounded by serpents and is now regarded only as a heavenly body under whose influence prophets and physicians are born. Through this elevation to the stars, the serpent-god becomes a transfigured totem. He is the cosmic father of those born in the month when his visibility is highest. In ancient astrology, mathematics and magic converge. The serpent figure in the heavens, found also in the constellation of the Great Serpent, is used as a mathematical outline; the points of luminosity are linked together by way of an earthly image, in order to render comprehensible an infinity we cannot comprehend at all without some such outline of orientation. So Asclepius is at once a mathematical border sign and a fetish bearer. The evolution of culture toward the age of reason is marked in the same measure as the tangible, coarse texture of life, fading into mathematical abstraction.

About twenty years ago in the north of Germany, on the Elbe, I found a strange example of the elementary indestructability of the memory of the serpent cult, despite all efforts of religious enlightenment; an example that shows the path on which the pagan serpent wanders, linking us to the past. On an excursion to the Vierlande [near Hamburg], in a Protestant church in Lüdingworth, I discovered, adorning the so-called rood screen, Bible illustrations that clearly originated in an Italian illustrated Bible and that had found their way here through the hands of a strolling painter.

And here I suddenly spotted Laocoon with his two sons in the terrible grasp of the serpent. How did he come to be in this church? But this Laocoon found his salvation. How? Looming in front of him was the staff of

Asclepius and on it a holy serpent, corresponding to what we read in the fourth book of the Pentateuch: that Moses had commanded the Israelites in the wilderness to heal snakebites by setting up a brazen serpent for devotion.

We have here a remnant of idolatry in the Old Testament. We know, however, that this can only be a subsequent insertion, intended to account retroactively for the existence of such an idol in Jerusalem. For the principal fact remains that a brazen serpent idol was destroyed by King Hezekiah under the influence of the prophet Isaiah. The prophets fought most bitterly against idolatrous cults that engaged in human sacrifice and worshipped animals, and this struggle forms the crux of Oriental and of Christian reform movements down to the most recent times. Clearly the setting up of the serpent is in starkest contradiction to the Ten Commandments, in sharpest opposition to the hostility to images that essentially motivates the reforming prophets.

But there is another reason why every student of the Bible should consider the serpent the most provocative symbol of hostility: the serpent on the tree in Paradise dominates the biblical narrative of the order of the world as the cause of evil and of sin. In the Old and New Testaments alike, the serpent clutches the tree of Paradise as the satanic power that summons the entire tragedy of sinning humanity as well as its hope for redemption.

In the battle against pagan idolatry, early Christianity was more uncompromising in its view of the serpent cult. In the eyes of the pagans, Paul was an impervious emissary when he hurled the viper that had bitten him into the fire without dying of the bite. (The poisonous viper belongs in the fire!) So durable was the impression of Paul's invulnerability to the vipers of Malta that as late as the sixteenth century, jugglers wound snakes around themselves at festivals and fairgrounds, representing themselves as men of the house of Saint Paul and selling soil from Malta as an antidote to snakebites. Here the prin-

IMAGES FROM THE REGION OF THE PUEBLO INDIANS

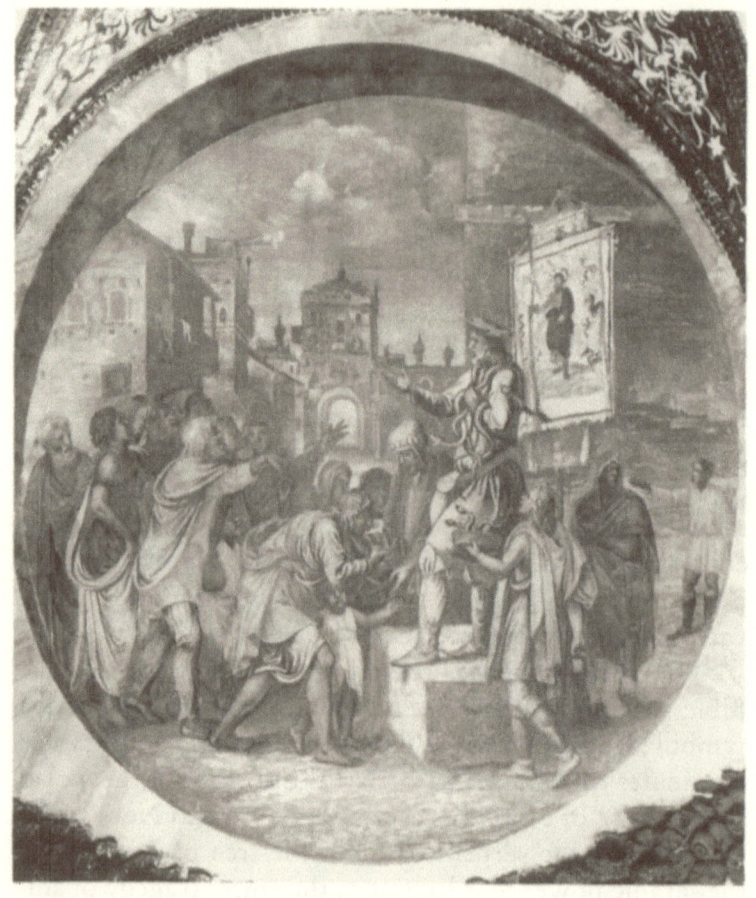

Fig. 27. Giulio Romano, Vendor of Antidote against Snakebite. Museo Civico Palazzo del Té, Mantua. Alinari/Art Resource, N. Y.

ciple of the immunity of the strong in faith ends up again in superstitious magical practice (*Figure 27*).

In medieval theology we find the miracle of the brazen serpent curiously retained as a part of legitimate religious devotion. Nothing attests to the indestructibility of the animal cult as does the survival of the miracle of the brazen serpent into the medieval Christian world view. So lasting in medieval theological memory was the serpent

ABY M. WARBURG

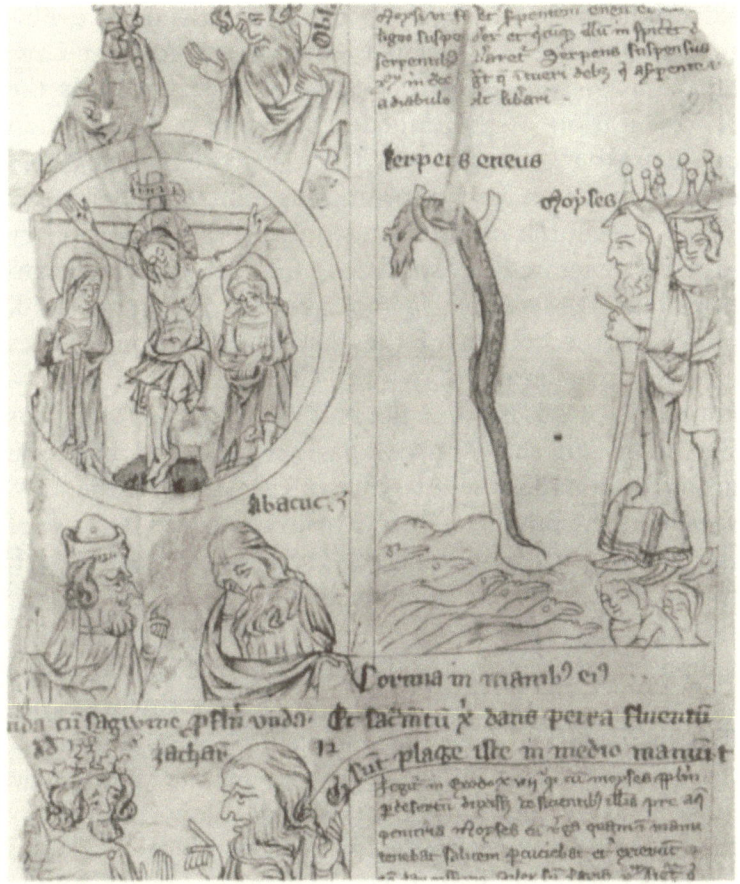

Fig. 28. Serpent and Crucifixion from *Speculum humanae salvationis.*
(By permission of the British Library, Add. Ms. 31303.)

cult and the need to overcome it that, on the basis of a
completely isolated passage inconsistent with the spirit
and the theology of the Old Testament, the image of serpent devotion became paradigmatic in typological representations for the Crucifixion itself (*Figure 28*). The animal image and the staff of Asclepius as reverential objects
for the kneeling multitude are treated and represented as
a stage, albeit to be overcome, in humanity's quest for

IMAGES FROM THE REGION OF THE PUEBLO INDIANS

salvation. In the attempt at a tripartite scheme of evolution and of the ages—that is, of Nature, Ancient Law, and Grace—an even earlier stage in this process is the representation of the impeded sacrifice of Isaac as an analogue to the Crucifixion. This tripartite scheme is still evident in the imagery adorning the minster of Salem.

In the church of Kreuzlingen itself, this evolutionary idea has generated an astonishing parallelism, which cannot make ready sense to the theologically uninitiated. Here, on the ceiling of the famous Mount of Olives chapel, immediately above the Crucifixion, we find an adoration of this most pagan idol with a degree of pathos that does not suffer in comparison with the Laocoon group. And under the reference to the Tables of the Law, which, as the Bible recounts, Moses destroyed because of the worship of the golden calf, we find Moses himself, forced into service as shield bearer to the serpent.

I shall be satisfied if these images from the everyday and festive lives of the Pueblo Indians have convinced you that their masked dances are not child's play, but rather the primary pagan mode of answering the largest and most pressing questions of the Why of things. In this way the Indian confronts the incomprehensibility of natural processes with his will to comprehension, transforming himself personally into a prime causal agent in the order of things. For the unexplained effect, he instinctively substitutes the cause in its most tangible and visible form. The masked dance is danced causality.

If religion signifies bonding,[5] then the symptom of evolution away from this primal state is the spiritualization of the bond between humans and alien beings, so that man no longer identifies directly with the masked symbol but, rather, generates that bond through thought alone, progressing to a systematic linguistic mythology. The will to devotional zeal is an ennobled form of the donning of a mask. In the process that we call cultural progress, the being exacting this devotion gradually loses its monstrous concreteness and, in the end, becomes a spiritualized, invisible symbol.

What does this mean? In the realm of mythology the law of the smallest unit does not hold; there is no search for the smallest agent of rationality in the course of natural phenomena; rather, a being saturated with as much demoniac power as possible is postulated for the sake of a true grasp of the causes of mysterious occurrences. What we have seen this evening of the symbolism of the serpent should give us at least a cursory indication of the passage from a symbolism whose efficacy proceeds directly from the body and the hand to one that unfolds only in thought. The Indians actually clutch their serpents and treat them as living agents that generate lightning at the same time that they represent lightning. The Indian takes the serpent in his mouth to bring about an actual union of the serpent with the masked figure, or at least with the figure painted as a serpent.

In the Bible the serpent is the cause of all evil and as such is punished with banishment from Paradise. Nevertheless, the serpent slithers back into a chapter of the Bible itself as an indestructible pagan symbol—as a god of healing.

In antiquity the serpent likewise represents the quintessence of the most profound suffering in the death of Laocoon. But antiquity is capable also of transmuting the inconceivable fertility of the serpent-deity, representing Asclepius as a savior and as the lord of the serpent, ultimately placing him—the serpent-god with the tamed serpent in his hand—as a starry divinity in the heavens.

In medieval theology, the serpent draws from this passage in the Bible the ability to reappear as a symbol of fate. Its elevation—though expressly considered as an evolutionary stage that has been surpassed—posits it on par with the Crucifixion.

In the end the serpent is an international symbolic

IMAGES FROM THE REGION OF THE PUEBLO INDIANS

answer to the question Whence come elementary destruction, death, and suffering into the world? We saw in Lüdingworth how christological thought makes use of pagan serpent imagery to express symbolically the quintessence of suffering and redemption. We might say that where helpless human suffering searches for redemption, the serpent as an image and explanation of causality cannot be far away. The serpent deserves its own chapter in the philosophy of "as if."

How does humanity free itself from this enforced bonding with a poisonous reptile to which it attributes a power of agency? Our own technological age has no need of the serpent in order to understand and control lightning. Lightning no longer terrifies the city dweller, who no longer craves a benign storm as the only source of water. He has his water supply, and the lightning serpent is diverted straight to the ground by a lightning conductor. Scientific explanation has disposed of mythological causation. We know that the serpent is an animal that must succumb, if humanity wills it to. The replacement of mythological causation by the technological removes the fears felt by primitive humanity. Whether this liberation from the mythological world view is of genuine help in providing adequate answers to the enigmas of existence is quite another matter.

The American government, like the Catholic Church before it, has brought modern schooling to the Indians with remarkable energy. Its intellectual optimism has resulted in the fact that the Indian children go to school in comely suits and pinafores and no longer believe in pagan demons. That also applies to the majority of educational goals. It may well denote progress. But I would be loath to assert that it does justice to the Indians who think in images and to their, let us say, mythologically anchored souls.

I once invited the children of such a school to illus-

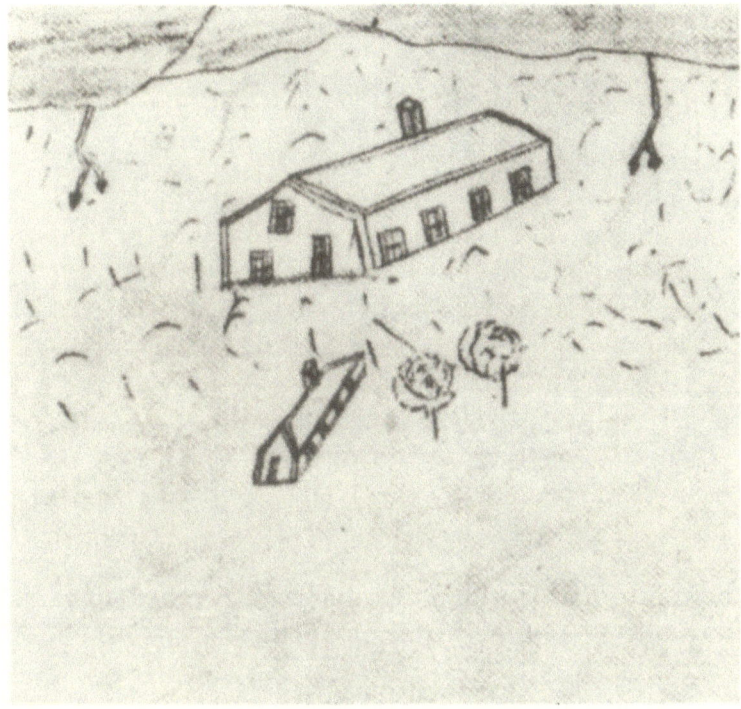

Fig. 29. Hopi schoolboy's drawing of a house in a storm with lightning.

trate the German fairy tale of "Johnny-Head-in-the-Air" (*Hans-Guck-in-die-Luft*), which they did not know, because a storm is referred to and I wanted to see if the children would draw the lightning realistically or in the form of the serpent. Of the fourteen drawings, all very lively but also under the influence of the American school, twelve were drawn realistically. But two of them depicted indeed the indestructible symbol of the arrow-tongued serpent, as it is found in the kiva (*Figure 29*).

We, however, do not want our imagination to fall under the spell of the serpent image, which leads to the primitive beings of the underworld. We want to ascend to

IMAGES FROM THE REGION OF THE PUEBLO INDIANS

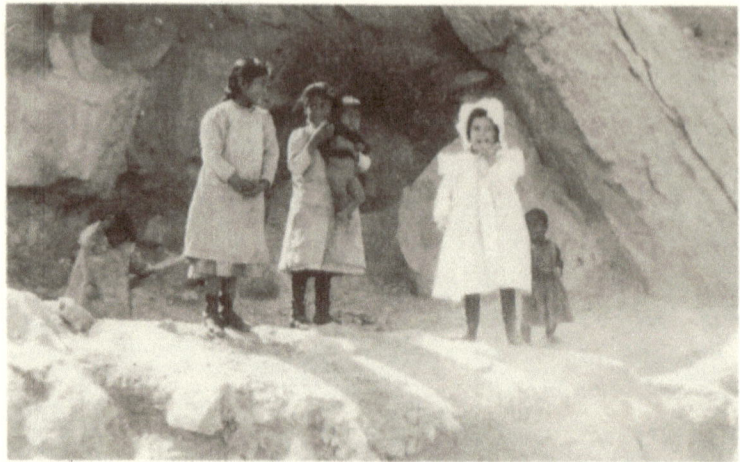

Fig. 30. "Children stand before a cave."

the roof of the worldhouse, our heads perched upwards in recollection of the words of Goethe:

Wär nicht das Auge sonnenhaft—
Die Sonne könnt' es nie erblicken.

If the eye were not of the sun,
It could not behold the sun.

All humanity stands in devotion to the sun. To claim it as the symbol that guides us upward from nocturnal depths is the right of the savage and the cultivated person alike. Children stand before a cave (*Figure 30*). To lift them up to the light is the task not only of American schools but of humanity in general.

The relation of the seeker of redemption to the serpent develops, in the cycle of cultic devotion, from coarse, sense-based interaction to its transcendence. It is and has always been, as the cult of the Pueblo Indians has shown, a significant criterion in the evolution from instinctual, magical interaction to a spiritualized taking of

ABY M. WARBURG

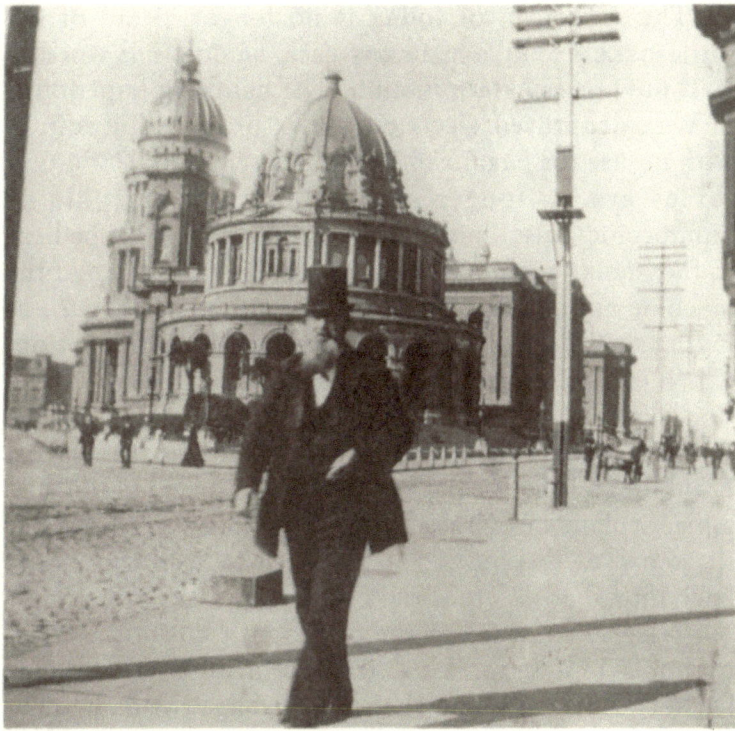

Fig. 31. "Uncle Sam."

distance. The poisonous reptile symbolizes the inner and outer demoniac forces that humanity must overcome. This evening I was able to show you all too cursorily an actual survival of the magical serpent cult, as an example of that primordial condition of which the refinement, transcendence, and replacement are the work of modern culture.

The conqueror of the serpent cult and of the fear of lightning, the inheritor of the indigenous peoples and of the gold seeker who ousted them, is captured in a photograph I took on a street in San Francisco. He is Uncle Sam in a stovepipe hat, strolling in his pride past a neoclassical rotunda. Above his top hat runs an electric wire. In this copper serpent of Edison's, he has wrested lightning from nature (*Figure 31*).

IMAGES FROM THE REGION OF THE PUEBLO INDIANS

The American of today is no longer afraid of the rattlesnake. He kills it; in any case, he does not worship it. It now faces extermination. The lightning imprisoned in wire—captured electricity—has produced a culture with no use for paganism. What has replaced it? Natural forces are no longer seen in anthropomorphic or biomorphic guise, but rather as infinite waves obedient to the human touch. With these waves, the culture of the machine age destroys what the natural sciences, born of myth, so arduously achieved: the space for devotion, which evolved in turn into the space required for reflection.

The modern Prometheus and the modern Icarus, Franklin and the Wright brothers, who invented the dirigible airplane, are precisely those ominous destroyers of the sense of distance, who threaten to lead the planet back into chaos.

Telegram and telephone destroy the cosmos. Mythical and symbolic thinking strive to form spiritual bonds between humanity and the surrounding world, shaping distance into the space required for devotion and reflection: the distance undone by the instantaneous electric connection.

ABY M. WARBURG

Notes

1. E. Schmidt, *Vorgeschichte Nordamerikas im Gebiet der Vereinigten Staaten*, 1894.

2. Jesse Walter Fewkes, "Archeological Expedition to Arizona in 1895," in *Seventeenth Annual Report of the Bureau of American Ethnology, 1895–96* (Washington, D.C., 1898), 2:519–74.

3. Πότνια Θηρῶν; see Jane E. Harrison, *Prolegomena to the Study of Greek Religion* (Cambridge, 1922), p. 264.

4. [Note from the 1988 German edition— M.P.S.] In the first draft of this passage, Warburg explained the symbolic power of the serpent image in the following way:

> Through which qualities does the serpent appear in literature and art as a usurping imposter [ein verdrängender Vergleicher]?
>
> 1. It experiences through the course of a year the full life cycle from deepest, deathlike sleep to the utmost vitality.
>
> 2. It changes its slough and remains the same.
>
> 3. It is not capable of walking on feet and remains capable nonetheless of propelling itself with great speed, armed with the absolutely deadly weapon of its poisonous tooth.
>
> 4. It is minimally visible to the eye, especially when its colors act according to the desert's laws of mimicry, or when it shoots out from its secret holes in the earth.
>
> 5. Phallus.
>
> These are qualities which render the serpent unforgettable as a threatening symbol of the ambivalent in nature: death and life, visible and invisible, without prior warning and deadly on sight.

5. Lactantius, *Divinae institutiones* 4.28.

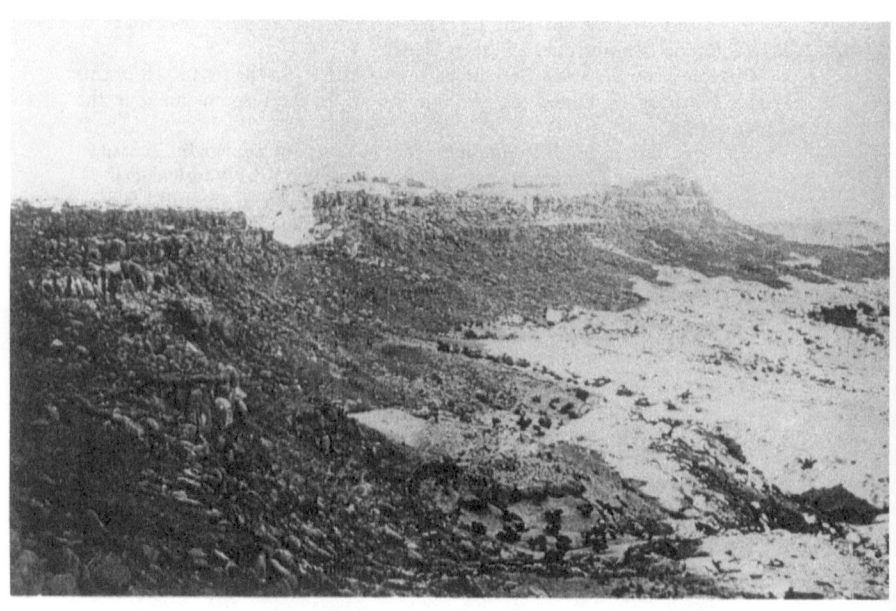

Fig. 32. Second Mesa, Hopi, Arizona. Photograph from the Warburg Archive.

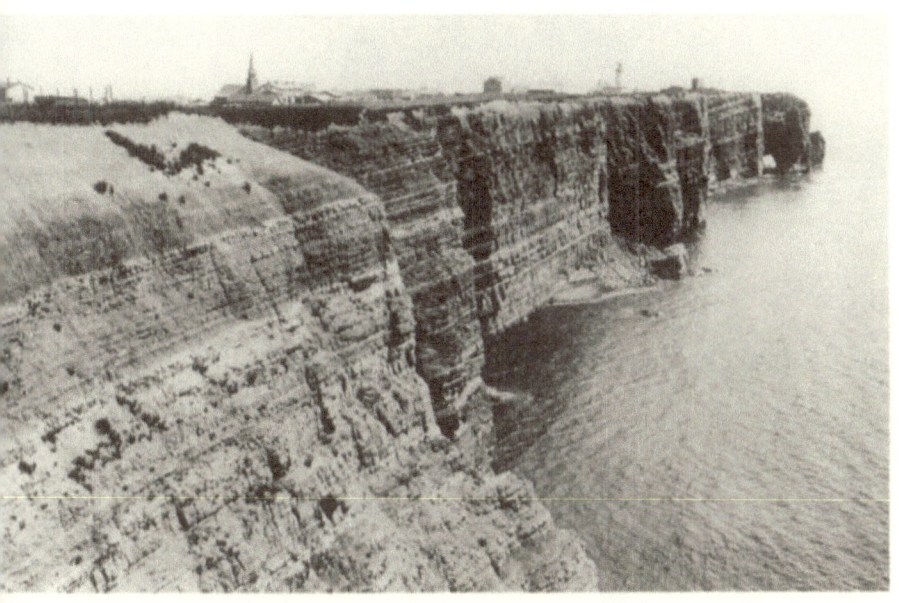

Fig. 33. Heligoland. Postcard from the Warburg Archive.

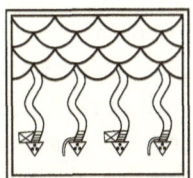

Aby Warburg's Kreuzlingen Lecture: A Reading

Il Fanciullo del West

The story is by now famous. In September 1895, the young art historian Aby Warburg left Florence for New York to attend the wedding of his brother Paul. He had much work planned during his projected three-year stay in Italy, which had begun the previous year, and there is no apparent evidence that he intended his American trip to be a long one. Curiously, his distaste for New York and the society to which he was introduced there served to prolong his American journey and make it into an episode of profound importance to his work and life.

In 1897, Warburg recalled his impression of New York in terms of the "practical foundation of this overrichly assorted, largest department store in the world." Paul Warburg's marriage to Nina Loeb reinforced the alliance of two prominent investment banks: M. M. Warburg of Hamburg and Kuhn-Loeb of New

York.[1] This world in itself was one from which Aby Warburg had fled already as a child. In 1923—the crucial year for the textual reconstruction of his American memories—he referred to the "emptiness of civilization in the American east" as the motivation for his "escape to the natural object and to scholarship."[2] The westward escape from New York thus recapitulated Warburg's life path and its two inner exiles: away from banking and away from established modes of art historical scholarship.

Warburg's American destination became the pueblos of the Native American Southwest. As E. H. Gombrich observed in his biography, Warburg's distaste for gilded American modernity fit into a larger, developing discomfort with the formalist modes of art history in which he had been trained. At this early point in his career, he seems to have begun to formulate ideas of the conjunctions between the production of culture itself and of aesthetic and symbolic images in particular. Thus the desire to reintegrate the viewing of art into the interpretation of culture led to the retrieval of the phenomenon of cultural production in "primitive" society. In his notes of 1923, and in a somewhat condescending remark on the attitudes of his own youth, Warburg added that "the will to the Romantic" had contributed to his westward fever.[3]

Gombrich suggests further that Warburg may have been influenced by the Berlin ethnologist Adolf Bastian, who had recently warned that "native cultures all over the world were in decline and if the material for a study of primitive man was not collected now, it would be irretrievably lost."[4] Bastian is the source of the concepts of the *Elementargedanke* (elementary thought or thinking) and the *Völkergedanke* (the thought or thinking of a people or nation). These categories generated Carl Jung's more famous notions of the archetype and the manifestation. We have here the basis of two directions in modern cultural anthropology: the cultural universalism associated with structural anthropology (Lévi-Strauss, with the

possible exception of *La pensée sauvage*) and the evolutionism that looks to "primitive" cultures for a shared
proximity to a pure and prehistorical cultural ground
zero (Frazer, Freud, and Eliade). In the 1890s, Warburg
was operating within this evolutionary framework. Another distinction, equally important, presents itself as
well: that between liberal and romantic evolutionism. To
Frazer and Freud, evolutionism meant the transcendence
of primitivism qua cultural barbarism. To Jung and
Eliade, evolutionism meant the loss of something pre-
cious and authentic. Warburg's early evolutionism implies the first— the liberal—agenda, but the evolutionism
itself does not last. "Images from the Region of the
Pueblo Indians" offers his new perspective, which took a
lifetime to generate.

Warburg's American itinerary took form through a
series of personal meetings and connections. His
brother's new wife was the sister of James Loeb (later the
founder of the Loeb Classical Library), who invited
Warburg to visit Harvard. An initial interest in Dakota
Indian wall paintings took him to Harvard's Peabody
Museum and onward to Washington and the
Smithsonian. Cyrus Adler, the Smithsonian's librarian,
professor of Semitic languages at Johns Hopkins, and an
acquaintance of the Loeb and Schiff families, introduced
him to Jesse Walter Fewkes and F. W. Hodge, and James
Mooney, who in turn introduced him to Frank Hamilton
Cushing. In New York he also met Franz Boas, whose
own German-Jewish origin provided an additional point
of contact. Adler showed Warburg ceramics that Fewkes
had removed from Hopi; Cushing spoke with him about
the symbolic ornamentation on the pottery; and Mooney
first told him about the Hopi snake dance.[5]

The contact with Mooney proved the most enduring,
and it might be fair to speculate as to the intellectual reason for this. In 1892–93, Mooney had published, in the
Annual Report of the Bureau of American Ethnology, his

study "The Ghost Dance Religion and the Sioux Outbreak of 1890." In it he discussed Sioux religion in a comparative context with other world religions: "The doctrines of the Hindu avatar, the Hebrew Messiah, the Christian millennium, and the Hesûnanin of the Indian Ghost Dance are essentially the same."[6] In the words of Anthony Wallace, "Mooney anticipated those later formulations which posit an essential processual similarity in revolutionary religious movements diverse in form and philosophical basis."[7]

Claudia Naber has recently reconstructed Warburg's American itinerary with great specificity.[8] At the Peabody, as she relates, Warburg found two sources on buffalo wall paintings in the Dakotas: George Catlin's 1841 *Letters and Notes on the Manners, Customs, and Conditions of the North American Indians* and Maximilian Prinz zu Wied's 1839–41 *Reise in das innere Nord-america in den Jahren 1832–1834*.[9] At the Smithsonian, on 23 October 1895, Warburg read G. E. A. Nordenskjöld's 1893 *The Cliff Dwellers of the Mesa Verde*, the work he described in 1923 as the inspiration for his travels to the American West. The cliff dwellings of the Anasazi had been discovered in 1888 by Richard Wetherill, a rancher and amateur archaeologist, whose Colorado home became Warburg's first western destination.[10]

Warburg left Washington at the beginning of November and traveled via Chicago and Denver. He says in his notes of 1923 that the firm of Kuhn-Loeb had procured for him, during his stay in Washington, letters of introduction from the ministers of war and of the interior. In Chicago, he presented a letter of introduction signed by a certain Mr. Seligmann to "the railroad magnate Robinson" and received a pass for free travel on the Mexican Central Railway, as well as a recommendation to the governor of New Mexico and to other "prominent people in the region of the Pueblo Indians" and a request

MICHAEL P. STEINBERG

for free passage on the Atchison–Topeka–Santa Fe railroad.[11] His documents introduced him as a "German scientist" and a "man of means."[12]

Warburg was guided through the Mesa Verde cliff
dwellings—the American Pompeii, as he described them
in a letter to his mother and sister written from Santa Fe
on 14 December 1895—by John Wetherill, Richard's
brother. (Richard was in New Mexico at the time, trading
for Indian objects.) From Mesa Verde, Warburg traveled
into New Mexico and visited the pueblos of San Juan,
Laguna, Acoma, Cochiti, and San Ildefonso. He observed
the antelope dance while at San Ildefonso. February and
March of 1896 he spent in California, enjoying his lei-
sure—for example, a stay at the Coronado Beach Hotel
(opened in 1888)—but also preparing for a springtime
return to the pueblos. As well, he visited the newly
founded campuses of Stanford University and the University of California at Berkeley.

At Stanford, Warburg had several discussions on
Hegel and F. T. Vischer with Julius Goebel, a German-
born professor of literature; and through Goebel he was
introduced to Earl Barnes, a pioneer in the study of child
psychology. Barnes had spent time in the early 1890s con-
ducting experiments on childhood creativity with stu-
dents in the California elementary schools. He would
first read aloud, from the *Struwwelpeter* stories, the
"Johnny-Head-in-the-Air" excerpt in which little Hans
falls into a creek during a storm; then he would ask the
children to illustrate the story. Warburg latched on to the
specific image of the storm and later conducted the same
experiment with Hopi schoolchildren.[13] Throughout his
western journey, Warburg kept notebooks and sketch-
books, which he filled with glossaries of Native American
terms, phrases, and bibliography as well as with drawings of symbols, costumes, and gestures.[14]

At the end of March 1896, Warburg returned from
California to the Southwest, arriving first in New Mexico

at Fort Wingate, visiting Zuñi, and then proceeding to Arizona—to Walpi and Oraibi and then to Keams Canyon, near the Hopi mesas. In 1923, Warburg recalled that "twenty-eight years ago the railroads did not yet affect the Moki [Hopi] villages." He recalled that outsiders were still welcome in these villages because the three days' distance between the railroad and the villages still left the Hopi with a sense of protective isolation.[15] Oraibi was at this time the only village on the mesas, and it was the dwelling place from 1893 to 1902 of the Mennonite missionary the Reverend H. R. Voth. Voth had gained wide access to Hopi rituals, access that included the permission to photograph, even inside the ceremonial kivas. Warburg stayed with him from 22 April to 2 May 1896, and Voth served as Warburg's guide. Through him, Warburg gained permission to photograph the humiskachina (corn) dances.[16] In Voth's company, he had even been allowed to enter the ceremonial kiva in Oraibi, on the eve of the humiskachina dance.[17] Warburg left the region at the beginning of May and in fact never observed the snake dance around which he later constructed his writing about the Hopi.

The central episode of Warburg's visit to the Hopi was his administration of Earl Barnes's experiment on a group of fourteen Hopi children at the Indian Service School at Keams Canyon on 24 April 1896. Following Barnes's model, Warburg told the children the story of "Johnny-Head-in-the-Air": "It was a dark cloudy day with much lightning. A mother told her little boy not to go out, but he went out into the storm. The storm became so terrible that he turned back, fell over a dog that he did not see and stumbled into a pond where his father found him and got him out with a long pole."[18] He then asked the children to draw an image of the storm, with lightning. Warburg's purpose was not, like Barnes's, to measure creativity but rather to explore, through the imagery of the children, the manifestation of the "primitive"

MICHAEL P. STEINBERG

imagination as conceived according to the criterion of the production of symbols. He was interested in seeing how the children drew the lightning: would they draw a naturalistic representation in the form of some kind of crooked line, or would they draw the Hopi lightning *symbol*—the serpent with a forked tongue—and thereby fail to distinguish the signifier from the signified? Warburg's working paradigm, which combined the study of art with a certain cultural anthropology, had clearly begun to develop but was still at an early stage. His dialogue with the Hopi was clearly motivated by a notion that the birth of modern culture and, a fortiori, of the modern cultural production of religious and aesthetic images, which in the Western tradition occurred in the culture and art of Quattrocento Florence, coincided with the mental and cultural capacity for the production of symbols. A rational symbolic practice separates signifier from signified, hence denotes the mental separation of human understanding and representation from the hidden actions of the divine, and ultimately serves as the foundation for the increasing psychological distance (*Distanz*) of the human imagination from the divine. This cultural phenomenon of increasing distance produced—in a linear view of the Western historical process of modernity—the Reformation and modern European secularization. In a fairly muddled convergence of the "primitive" and the child, Warburg thought to measure the path to modernity by the path to symbolization: the fewer serpents and the more zigzags, the more advanced the ability to identify a ritual symbol (the serpent) as such and to separate it from a nonceremonial image of a physical phenomenon: a lightning strike, representable, presumably, by a zigzag. The more rational (i.e., systematic) the symbolic practice, the more modern the mind—both onto- and phylogenetically speaking, presumably—at work. (It does not seem to have occurred to Warburg that Hopi cultural perception—adult or child—might not categorize a physical phenomenon outside the context of ritual representation.) The results of Warburg's experiment made sense to him: twelve of the fourteen children drew zigzags; two drew serpents (see *Figure 29*). In Warburg's 1896 conceptualization, therefore, Hopi culture was on the road from primitivism to rationality and modernity.

As far as Warburg's conceptualizations of 1896 are concerned, the question of to what extent the idea of modernization through symbolic form either generated the dialogue with Hopi culture or was generated by it is very difficult to answer. In his notes to the lecture on the Hopi serpent ritual, which he prepared in the Kreuzlingen sanatorium for 21 April 1923, Warburg stated the importance to his subsequent work of his American journey. Although we cannot know where and how to draw the line, we have to allow for the separation—distance—between his actions of 1896 and his recollections of 1923: "I did not yet realize that, as a result of my American journey, the organic connection between the art and the religion of 'primitive' peoples would become so clear to me, so that I could see so clearly the identity, or rather the indestructibility of primitive man— who remains the same in all times, so that I could draw him out as an organic entity precisely in the culture of early Renaissance Florence and, later, in the German Reformation."[19] In a blunter statement of the same sentiment, Warburg wrote, in English, on 17 May 1907, to James Mooney of the Smithsonian:

> I receive the Reports of your admirable Institution, but I have not very often time enough to read them because my studies are once again the Renaissance period. Nevertheless I always feel myself very much indebted to your Indians. Without the study of their primitive (?) civilization I never would have been able to find a larger basis for the Psychology of the Renaissance. One day or other I shall

send you a specimen of my method, which, I dare say, is
new and therefore, perhaps, not as far acknowledged as I
could expect. Nevertheless I work without losing the belief
in the unknown master who directs our attention.[20]

The question mark after the word *primitive* is Warburg's,
and it is a significant signal. His recategorization of the
"primitive" developed during the writing of the Kreuzlingen lecture in the spring of 1923.

The second and third sections of this essay therefore
address two biographical issues: first, the significance of
the return of the youthful experiences in the American
Southwest to the mind and work of Aby Warburg during
his darkest period, the years of institutionalization in
Ludwig Binswanger's Kreuzlingen sanatorium, the
"Heilanstalt Bellevue," from 1921 to 1924; and second,
the autobiographical memory Warburg chose to invoke
in 1923 and the broken process through which the resonances of Hopi paganism served and haunted his later
scholarship.

Demons: Personal and Cultural

My purpose here is not to resketch Warburg's biography
(1866–1929) or to recast its foundations. Nevertheless,
as is well known, the conjunctions of personal and intellectual biography are decisive throughout his life and are
of particular importance when his own thinking about
issues of primitivism and rationality is at stake. Although
clinical information has not been available to his biogra-
phers, it has been a general assumption that Warburg
lived on the border of mental illness through much of his
life and that a short-term etiology of unknown character
preceded his breakdown in late 1918 and the subsequent
institutionalization, which lasted until 1924. His main
biographer, E. H. Gombrich, has treated this problem in

Warburg's biography with care and with the charge that
"it does not lie within the scope or the competence of this
study to describe the mental agonies of Warburg's psy-
chotic years. No more need be said, at any rate, than that
the inferno into which he descended should not be ro-
manticized."[21]

The problematic effect of this fundamentally sensible
charge, however, has been the tendency to duplicate
Warburg's lifelong battle against his "demons" on the
level of his intellectual work. In other words, the tendency has been to look at Warburg's view of culture in
terms of his alleged projection of a straightforward path
from the primitive, the pagan, and the irrational to the
modern and the rational. This is a questionable model for
examining Warburg's thought (including the relation between his work and his own psyche); for it is a model of
repression rather than one of "working through." It is
Gombrich's model, and it alludes, silently, to his own
Popperian positivism and—a fortiori—to his antipathy to
psychoanalytic constructs. The same assumption makes
its way into George Mosse's elegant summary of
Warburg's work: "For Aby Warburg, scholarship was a
way to maintain rationality in an increasingly complex
and irrational world, a means of maintaining control in a
world bordering on chaos—to warn, to exorcise, to en-
courage, never detached from the challenge of the
times."[22]

Because Warburg liked mottoes, one of his most famous has regularly been used, abused, and mistranslated
to reinforce this repressive view of his cultural practice.
His great (perhaps his greatest) essay of 1918–19 (published in 1920), "Heidnisch-antike Weissagung in Wort
und Bild zu Luthers Zeiten" (Pagan-ancient prophecy in
word and image in Luther's times) contains the following
passage (cited by Gombrich, but duplicated here with my
own translation):

Die Wiederbelebung der dämonischen Antike vollzieht sich dabei, wie wir sahen, durch eine Art polarer Funktion des einfühlenden Bildgedächtnisses. Wir sind im Zeitalter des Faust, wo sich der moderne Wissenschaftler—zwischen magischer Praktik und kosmologischer Mathematik—den Denkraum der Besonnenheit zwischen sich und dem Objekt zu erringen versuchte. Athen will eben immer wieder neu aus Alexandrien zurückerobert sein.

The reinvigoration of demoniac antiquity is accomplished, as we have seen, through a kind of polar function of empathic image-memory. We are in the age of Faust, in which the modern scholar—between magical practice and cosmological mathematics—strove to posit a space for enlightened reflection between himself and the object world. Athens always wants precisely to be reconquered anew from Alexandria.

There are many keywords here, perhaps chief among them *Denkraum* (the space for reflection), the value threatened by modernization which Warburg invokes at the end of the Kreuzlingen lecture. Gombrich follows his citation with a poigant plea that this passage be read for its "tragic awareness of the threat which the powers of fear and of primitive magic mentality constitute to the realm of reason and reflection." He states also that its pathos must be absorbed from "the original German." Yet Gombrich's own passion for reason seems unable to perceive the passage's painful ambivalence between, and simultaneity of, the primitive and the rational, "Alexandria" and "Athens." Curiously, he translates the last sentence as "Athens must always be conquered afresh from Alexandria."[23] Warburg speaks of the internal desire of Athens—what Athens wants, which is the continual desire to control the ongoing historical and psychological dialectic with Alexandria. In the definitions of the poles and the nature of their dialectic, we are in the shadow of

Nietzsche (the Apollonian and the Dionysian), where Popperians, apparently, fear to tread. The motto placed as the epigraph to the "Lecture on Serpent Ritual" published in 1939 echoes Warburg's intention: "Es ist ein altes Buch zu blättern, Athen-Oraibi, alles Vettern" (translated, without the rhyme: "It is the lesson from an old book: the kinship of Athens and Oraibi"). The motto comes from Goethe's *Faust*, Part 2. Warburg had used it in his Luther essay, in a different version: "Es ist ein altes Buch zu blättern, Vom Harz bis Hellas, alles Vettern." There, Germany and a notion of Germanic primitiveness are juxtaposed with Greece. Nowhere is it implied that kinship assures harmony.

The historical category that remains Warburg's life-long object of analysis is paganism. Often synonymous with primitivism, it is a term that Warburg tends to qualify with quotation marks—and at least in one instance with a question mark. Paganism is an "early" cultural phenomenon, but it returns as a dominant cultural mode at various historical moments, and it remains as a dormant potentiality both in cultural groups and in individual persons. A source of great inner conflict for Warburg was his intransigent insistence that Judaism retained a primitive, pagan presence in the modern world. His attitude and his scholarship on the question of paganism thus necessarily converged with his attitude toward Judaism, Jews, and his own Jewish identity. Paganism links his inner persona to the object-world of scholarship. There can be no assumption of distance between Warburg and the pagan world—despite or, rather, because of the fact that distance remains the elusive goal of modern rationality, cultural and personal.

This dialectic must be understood in terms of the psychoanalytic notion of working through and, in a complementary way, in terms of an emerging cultural phenomenology. The "Other" is both what is foreign in the self and what is culturally foreign. In the evolution of both

MICHAEL P. STEINBERG

aspects of Warburg's model, the scholarly as well as the inner, psychological resolution culminates in the writing of the Kreuzlingen lecture of April 1923. The *act* of writing is by no means a secondary element in this process; it is the lifelong conjunction of Warburg's psychological and scholarly energies. There are two points to be made here. First, his biography proceeds through his writings: letters, diaries, and scholarly texts. Thus his intellectual and personal biography needs to be traced in terms of the genealogy of texts. Second, the recovery (in a clinical sense) of the person is achieved through the writing of a text (the Kreuzlingen lecture), and that recovery is also the recovery of writing itself.

The mutuality of the subjectivity and mode of cultural analysis achieved through the writing of the Kreuzlingen lecture shows the mark of Ludwig Binswanger. In and beyond his association with Warburg, Binswanger is the figure where psychoanalysis and phenomenology converge. Indeed, the Binswanger-Warburg dialogue has rich potential for the as-yet-unwritten joint history of phenomenology and subjectivity. Binswanger had become director of the Kreuzlingen sanatorium in 1910, on the death of his father. He transformed its clinical profile immediately, integrating into its traditionally positivistic and physiologically oriented praxis a profound, but not uncritical, reception of Freudian psychoanalysis. Binswanger was critical of what he understood as the biologically drive-oriented composition of the Freudian personality and strove to treat and restore an existentially viable and complicated subjectivity. He thus advanced what has come to be referred to as existential psychology and existential phenomenology, with his own passion and significance increasing after the publication of Heidegger's *Being and Time* in 1927. His interaction with Warburg came in the post-Freudian, pre-Heideggerian period of his career and thus merits further exploration.[24]

In 1949, Binswanger published a study entitled *Henrik Ibsen and the Problem of Self-Realization in Art.* Although this publication belongs to a later period in his career, its theme expresses a model of selfhood that appears highly relevant to Warburg's own development during his years in Kreuzlingen. This model has been analyzed by Paul de Man in an essay called "Ludwig Binswanger and the Sublimation of the Self."[25] De Man describes this model of selfhood as

> that of the author as he is changed and interpreted by his work. . . . For Binswanger, the literary enterprise can nowhere be distinguished from the project of self-realization. . . . The expansion of the self seems to occur in and probably by means of the work. The authenticating function of the work that "elevates" the writer above his original identity is so fundamentally implicit in Binswanger's thought that he takes it entirely for granted, without feeling called upon to state it as a distinctive theme or thesis.[26]

Writing, and, more specifically, writing the lecture on the Hopi, became for Warburg an act of self-realization. Self-realization can be described in terms of sublimation, in the Freudian sense of the dynamic of the creative process, individual or collective. The therapeutic and asymmetric aspects of their association notwithstanding, there are noteworthy parallels in Warburg's and Binswanger's developing ideas of culture and subjectivity. Both questioned, in this period, the possibility and character of an individual subjectivity that would both be free of cultural and ideological coercion and, at the same time carry cultural content and connection. After 1927, Heidegger offered a new paradigm to existential phenomenology in the category of authenticity, or the rediscovery of Being.

Warburg's emerging cultural phenomenology, highly personal, autobiographically and indeed therapeutically implicated, at no point claimed to discover in theory or in personal experience a new cultural or personal authenticity. Indeed, the personal equilibrium Warburg attained after 1923 did not generate an equilibrated cultural theory that could integrate paganism and rationality. On the contrary, these categories never resolve their opposition. If my approach differs from the traditional one that sees a fortress rationality posited against cultural demons, I do not intend —with regard to Warburg's biography or to his scholarship—to advocate a romanticization or aestheticization of cultural or personal violence. Clearly, Warburg could never have shown the aestheticizing—and ultimately barbarous—complacency of Wagner's Hans Sachs, who stands at the source of a fulminating German and French desire for violence and aesthetic renewal, where cultural violence is necessary for artistic inspiration ("Nun schau'n wir wie Hans Sachs es macht, dass er den Wahn fein lenken kann, ein edles Werk zu tun").27 Just as the aestheticization of culture is precluded, so is the claim of resolution of cultural tension and conflict. The only Eden that Warburg ever sought or ever found, as we shall see at this essay's conclusion, was a hotel in Rome.

The 1923 lecture notes contain passages that justify the connections I am trying to draw. Warburg gives at least partial answers to three important questions: Why did he abandon the Hopi material for so long? Where did he first infer a connection between Hopi and Hebrew culture? And what is the nature of the recurring irrationality of culture which precludes a victory of modernizing rationality?

What I saw and experienced can be represented only in its outer appearance [Schein], and I have the right to speak about it only if I say first that its insoluble problematic has been so pressing a burden on my soul, that in my healthy time I never would have dared to say something scholarly about it.

But now, in March 1923, in Kreuzlingen, in a sealed institution, where I find myself a seismograph made of pieces of wood stemming from a growth transplanted from the Orient into the nourishing north-German plain while carrying a branch inoculated in Italy, I allow the signals that I have received to be released from me, because in this epoch of a chaotic defeat even the weakest one is beholden to strengthen the will to cosmic order.

This passage concludes the notes of 14 March; the following day's entries begin

The primitive culture [this phrase changed from "the artistic culture"] of the Pueblo Indians presents the rationalistically decadent European with an uneasy, painful and therefore unwelcome method of decisively destroying his belief in an idyllically mellow fairyland as the universal original home [*Urheimat*] of man before the fall from grace of the Enlightenment. The fairy-tale foundation in the practice and art of the Indians is a symptom and indication of a desperate search for order against chaos, and hardly a smug and self-contented self-abandon to the flow of things. A fairy-tale animal, appearing as the concretest product of playful fantasy is in statu nascendi an abstraction grasped with great effort. It determines the dimensions of phenomena that in their otherwise ephemeral intangibility cannot be seized. Example: the serpent dance of Oraibi.

The line Warburg draws here is a tragic, Weberian one: not between primitivism and rationality but between a dangerous enchantment and a decayed rationality. He chooses neither. The notes of 15 March end with a discussion of the serpent dance as a desire for rain, and thus for food, but also as an expression of seasonal and generational continuity. "The founding category of causal thinking is filiation [*Kindschaft*]," he writes. The notes of the following day are taken up by autobiographical recollection of the 1875 illness of Warburg's mother (which is discussed in the next section). It is clearly possible that the previous day's reflections on generations are involved in this association. The notes of 17 March make a strong point that attempts to question the "iron cage" historical process suggested above:

> With primitive man, images of memory lead to religious activity[;] with civilized [man] to recorded sketches. All of mankind is eternally and for all time schizophrenic. But perhaps ontogenetically an attitude can be identified which sees these remembered images as prior and primitive and yet still present. At a later stage, the remembered image is evoked not as an unmediated, practical reflexive act—whether as warfare or religion; rather, the images are deliberately stored in pictures or signs. Between these two stages is the treatment, the experience of an impression, which can be called symbolic thinking.

The last extant note, dating from 29 March, contains the following assertion and association:

> The light volume of curious spectators notwithstanding, the fact of distance, destroyed by culture, must have an entirely different sort of destructive effect on the life of pagan religiosity. The adversity that the Indian of the empty steppes answers by planting corn flows forth in the same measure as the easy water supply or even irrigation of cultured lands. For the unfruitfulness of the ground in the absence of rainfall was and is the primal cause of religious magic among the Pueblo Indians. Desert and dryness [*Wüste und Wassernot*] function here as religion-creating factors in the same way as in the desert wandering of the Jews under Moses's leadership.

The juxtaposition of Pueblo Indians and ancient Hebrews

leaves one question unanswered: Which resulting Hebrew religious practice does Warburg have in mind here, Mosaic Judaism or the idolatry of the golden calf?

The Kreuzlingen Lecture on serpent ritual of 21 April 1923 resulted from the second legendary "business deal" Warburg made in his life. This negotiation was for his discharge from the sanatorium, on the condition that he prove able to give a sustained academic lecture. Thus the lecture's ostensible theme, that of the birth of rationality from paganism, on which he had worked throughout his scholarship on the Renaissance, had a personal refraction. (The first deal is well known: thirteen-year-old Aby offered his younger brother Max his birthright [Max's biblical image] to the business in exchange for the promise that his book collecting would always be funded. The result was the Warburg Library and the confession from Max Warburg—repeated at Aby's memorial service—that this subvention was the most reckless one of his life.[28])

The stakes of this second deal were higher for Warburg, presumably, than for his doctors. For them, the test of sanity was an hour's talk. For Warburg, it had to do with the lecture's theme. If he could revive the material on the Hopi, which—apart from the brief references quoted above—he had kept hidden and unresolved since 1897, and could finally articulate a position on the place of rationality in culture, then his own biography and his scholarly style, which had always been intertwined, would dictate the partnership of scholarly and personal resolution. The lecture notes he compiled in March 1923 thus conjure autobiographical episodes that from earliest youth commingle with the issues of pagan culture. The notes themselves waft in and out of coherence; show transparently the emotionally charged process of "working through" which they generate; and appear, certainly, as Warburg's own dance with the serpent.

MICHAEL P. STEINBERG

Autobiographical Conundrums, Recalled in 1923

Warburg's early biography, as reconstructed from correspondence and from the autobiographical elements of the
1923 lecture notes, points to a crucial but highly sensi-
tive, indeed tortured formula for the late-nineteenth-century German intellectual: the conviction that Judaism is
the cultural partner of paganism, not of rationality. An
acceptance of this formula in Warburg's lifelong thinking
makes the "fortress rationality" position untenable. In
question are both the fragmented subject and the diagno-
sis of Judaism in various historical manifestations—including even that of the Hamburg Jewish patriciate—as a
vestige of cultural primitivism. Warburg's desire for distance from contemporary religious practice recalls
Freud's. For Warburg as for Freud, the continuum from
the primitive and the irrational to the modern and the
rational was a fluid one. In the later cultural writings of
Freud, the cultural potential of this fluidity grew more
ominous; for Warburg it had always been a terrible
threat. On the personal level, Warburg never achieved a
secure distance from the same cultural demons; for Freud
this was not a concern. It seems clear that, in Warburg's
mind, the lecture on the serpent dance in April 1923 was
his own dance with the serpent, a coming to terms with
the two dialectics that had determined, and indeed under-
mined, his lifelong sensibility: primitivism, or paganism,
and rationality; and paganism and Judaism.

The preparatory lecture notes digress repeatedly into
autobiographical issues. Such references can be corrobo-
rated by a significant body of early correspondence.
Thus, in a recent article entitled "Aby Warburg in His
Early Correspondence," A. M. Meyer defined the issue:
"Exactly what was the relation between Warburg's research on paganism in the Renaissance and his media-
tions and fears about Judaism (and Jews) remains of

course the problem."[29] Meyer draws from the young Warburg's letters to his family to form a rich picture of the sensibilities of his personal crisis as well as of a more general crisis among the assimilated Jewry of Wilhelmine Germany. In the Warburg family, religious practice had become—certainly in Aby's eyes—formalistic. (As Meyer points out—correcting some recent conjecture—the young Aby Warburg did not read the Talmud in his childhood home and received no religious instruction from his father, the banker Moritz Warburg. Aby learned Hebrew from his mother.)[30] It thus presented a double danger: that which was inherent, for Warburg, in ritual paganism, as well as that of increased vulnerability to anti-Semitism. Meyer has shown clearly how severe this conflict became during the years of Warburg's intellectual formation.

In the 1923 lecture notes, Warburg recorded his earliest childhood memory as the demoniac dreams he suffered while ill with typhus at age six, in 1873. The imagery of these dreams was inspired, he speculates, from the illustration in Balzac's "Die kleinen Leiden des Ehestandes" (Petites misères de la vie conjugale), which had been read to him.[31] In the notes of the same day, he also discusses the second traumatic episode of his childhood: the illness of his mother in the summer of 1875, while vacationing in the Austrian resort of Ischl. He recalls being forced by his grandfather and a "Jewish-Austrian" tutor to say prayers for his mother and escaping from these rituals by consuming sausages (his first infraction of dietary law) from a local delicatessen and by reading stories of American Indians—in a volume he recalls, uncertainly, as *Eine Reise nach dem Westen* (A Journey to the West), by an author named Brown.[32] Warburg thus recalls his original "will to the Romantic" as a desire to escape from ritual (a predicament to be repeated in New York in 1895, after his brother's wedding festivities) and certainly not as the desire to find it.

MICHAEL P. STEINBERG

Warburg had completed his Realgymnasium at age eighteen and enrolled in the Gelehrtenschule des Johanneums for eighteen months to fulfill university entrance requirements. There, he read G. E. Lessing's *Laocoon* with Oscar Ohlendorff. Gombrich suggests that Lessing's argument for the necessity of restraint in visual modes of representation—the sigh of the sculptured figure of Laocoon as he is attacked by serpents, as opposed to the agonized screams in Virgil's poetic depiction—drew Warburg into the study of visual art. At the same time, Gombrich suggests that this turn to the study of images "must have seemed suspect to Warburg's orthodox relations."[33] Image versus word: Which is more primitive, more threatening? Which provides distance from ritual madness? Did the turn to the study of images signify an escape from the emotional dangers of word-centered Judaism? In a life of looking at images, Warburg was looking for, and looking at, the truth; and this truth consisted of personal, cultural, and historical conflicts and their representations. The question of Judaism remained present, if not often explicitly invoked. Warburg thus founds the practice of cultural iconology in a way that was immediately diminished by his successors. His iconology de-idolizes the image, makes it move, travels from the surface into the depths where dwell the demons personal, cultural, social, and political.

Between 1886 and 1889, Warburg was enrolled at the University of Bonn, where his teachers were Carl Justi and Henry Thode for the history of art, Reinhard Kekulé von Stradonitz for archaeology, Hermann Usener for classical mythology, and Karl Lamprecht for the philosophy of history. When urged by his grandparents to change universities because of his tendency to ignore dietary laws in Bonn, Warburg wrote to his father: "Since I do not arrange my course of study according to the quality of ritual restaurants but according to the quality of my teachers, I do not eat ritually."[34] He spent the winter of 1888–89 in Florence, working with August Schmarsow, professor of art history in Breslau, in preparation for the founding of a German art historical institute there. In October 1889 he moved to the University of Strassburg to study with Hubert Janitschek (art history), Adolf Michaelis (archaeology), and Theobald Ziegler (philosophy). In a letter of 25 November 1889, he wrote to his mother of his depression at the anti-Semitic barbs to which he was subjected; several times a day he heard voices in the street behind him saying, in Alsatian dialect, "Desch ischt e Jud" (That is a Jew).[35]

In 1897, Warburg married Mary Hertz, the Protestant daughter of a Hamburg senator. His parents did not attend the wedding but visited the couple in Wiesbaden just before their departure for Florence. The couple had three children, whom Mary took to church and whom Aby took to his mother's house for the Passover Seder, "providing," as A. M. Meyer relates, "rather irreverently, German nursery rhymes for the traditional Hebrew songs."[36]

The most difficult period in Warburg's personal negotiation with Judaism and Jewish ritual came with the death of his father in January 1910. He did not attend the funeral or fulfill the traditional duty of the eldest son to say the mourners' *Kaddish* at a later memorial service. As Meyer records, he wrote to his brother Max:

> The whole celebration acquires, in a natural and subjectively absolutely justified manner, the character of a demonstration for the faithful Jews. I do not wish to disturb this. I am after all in the eyes of others an unreliable customer, but in my own eyes a political opponent of clerical elementary schools such as the Talmud Torah School, and above all I am a 'Cherem' [banned] through my mixed marriage and as the father of non-denominational children whom I shall never lead to Judaism. . . . The Mourners' Kaddish is a matter for the eldest son: it signifies not only

an external act, but at this public memorial service demonstrates acceptance of the moral inheritance. I will not make myself guilty of such public hypocrisy. No one is entitled to demand this of me.

On 25 February, two days before the memorial service, Warburg wrote in his diary, as Meyer relates: "Still more: to rend one's clothes, to put on carpet slippers, to say *Kaddish*, morning and night, regardless of whether one is oneself again attacked by demons. . . . There is no style in this, especially if one respects Father. My respect for him lies in my not hushing up the absolute antithesis in *Weltanschauung* through an external cultic act: for I am dissident."[37] The nature of the relationship between demons and dissidence is hard to know, but it is not one of simple cause and effect, or of symptom and repression.

The years of the First World War were deeply agonizing for Warburg. They brought out profound conflicts and recurring demons and, according to most observers—including Gombrich—played a role in the mental aggravation that preceded the post-1918 breakdown. Like many intellectuals, Warburg saw the war as a crucible for German Jewry and as the end of the century of assimilated culture. He was not alone in suffering this inner conflict, but the fact that it was shared made it no less wrenching. He was conscious of, and not entirely unsympathetic to, the German patriotism that generated the war; yet at the same time he realized that the argument for German cultural superiority possessed an inherent anti-Semitism that would now, inevitably, intensify.

Warburg's agony is vividly manifest in the materials he collected during the war, in a file box marked "Juden." As is well known, he kept an elaborate system of notes, collected, ultimately, into well over a hundred file boxes, arranged by subject, which in their organization rival the idiosyncrasies of his library.[38] The box marked "Juden" (no. 36) contains a bibliographic section listing books by and about Jews, with an emphasis on works published during the war years; other subfiles labeled "Antisemitica," "Juden und Krieg" (Jews and war), and "Konfessionsfragen" (Religious questions); and a general section containing newspaper clippings and materials on the Warburg family as well as family correspondence.

Perhaps the most extraordinary material in this file box is a group of twenty picture postcards from a series called "Jüdische Kriegspostkarten" (Jewish war postcards) published during the war by the Lamm Verlag in Berlin. Bundled together without written comment by Warburg, the postcards express a clear propagandist message of German-Jewish solidarity on the war front as well as German and German-Jewish support for Polish and Russian Jewry against indigenous anti-Semitism. Several images show Jewish rituals observed on the Belgian and Russian fronts, including a Passover Seder in Saint-Quentin and a Yom Kippur service in Brussels, both photographed in 1915. Several show services held in the field, with makeshift arks constructed on sticks. One of these field services is an ecumenical one, described as a "konfessionelle Verbrüderung" (ecumenmical brotherhood) with an attending portrait of the Jewish, Catholic, and Evangelical clergy. As for the protection of eastern European Jewry, several images show vandalized Jewish cemeteries, with damaged headstones or with trenches dug, by the Russians, alongside the graves. One postcard depicts Torah scrolls in Sochaczew, destroyed by the Russians.

The iconographically most complicated images portray the relationships between the German forces and the "liberated" Jews. There are group identification photographs—marked as passport photographs—of Łódź Jews, one of a group of men, one of a group of women. The most arresting image of all is an intentionally allegorical one: entitled "Grosspolen unter deutschem

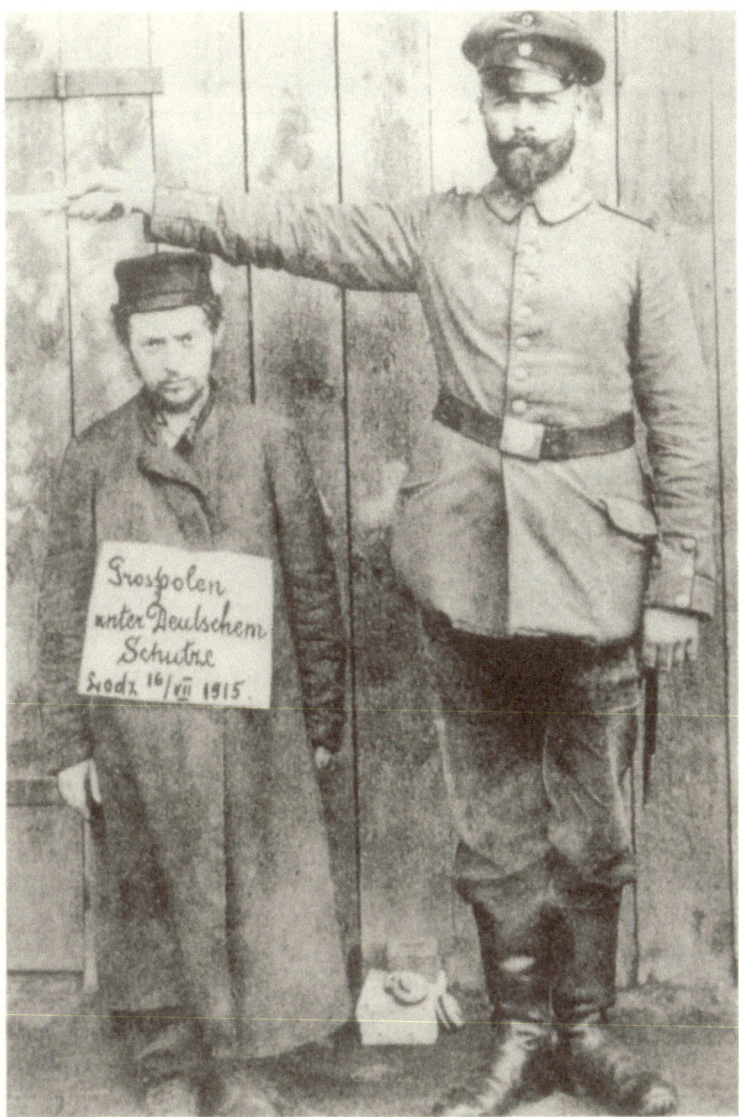

Fig. 34. "Grosspolen unter deutschem Schutze." From the series "Jüdische Kriegspostkarten," Lamm Verlag, Berlin. Warburg Archive.

ABY WARBURG'S KREUZLINGEN LECTURE

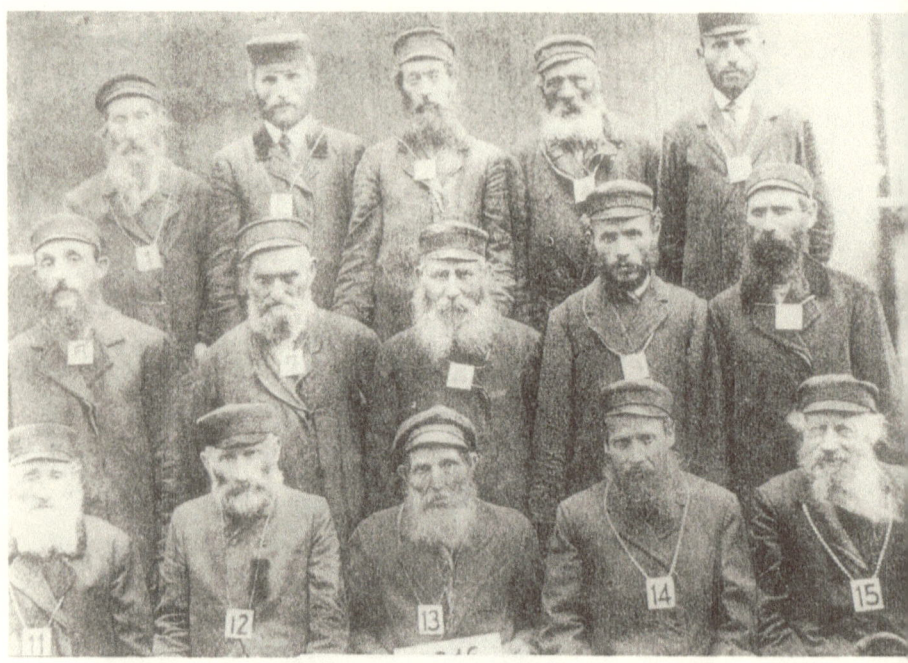

Fig. 35. Identification photograph of Jewish men in Łódź, 1915.

Schutze" (Greater Poland under German protection), it portrays a young, short-statured Jewish man in black garb, with a sign hanging on his chest marked "Grospolen [*sic*] unter deutschem Schutze, Lodz 16 VII 1915." Next to him stands a Prussian officer with an uncanny resemblance to William II, dressed in parade uniform and dress helmet (the "Paradehut"), holding an outstretched sword over the head of the Jew in a gesture of protection (*Figure 34*). The officer's expression is solemn; the Jew's, one of fear. The collective passport photographs, taken by the Germans to identify groups of Jews, reflect similar expressions of fear and suspicion (*Figure 35*). The indigenous Jews seem to mistrust or fear the eye of the camera as well as the attendant manifesta-

MICHAEL P. STEINBERG

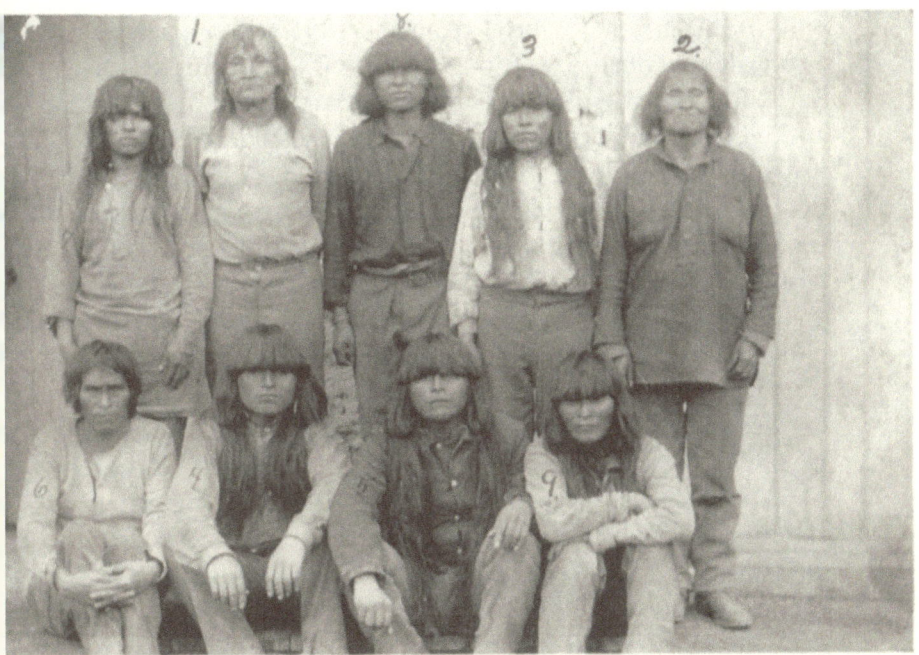

Fig. 36. Hostile Hopi (1905). Southwest Museum Collection.

tions of control and authority by the "liberating" German forces.

I now want to offer a speculation that I cannot support but that seems too resonant to withhold. Visually and iconographically, there is a clear resemblance between these photographs of Polish Jews taken by German army photographers and the portraits of Hopi Indians (*Figure 36*) taken by the Reverend H. R. Voth, some in the actual company of Aby Warburg. In both cases, the camera creates primitiveness by recording an asymmetric exchange between, on the side of the observers, a culture of expansion, power, control, and professed intentions of liberation and, on the side of the observed, a culture seen, literally, as primitive and transformable. My speculation is twofold: First, Warburg, from the 1895 trip on, senses a parallel between the Hopi and the Jews as primitives in an expanding world defined by economic, technological, and cultural modernization. The primitivism applies here not only to the Jews living in Polish villages, who were ordinarily not in his purview, but to the ritualistic residues present in the practices even of the Hamburg Jewish community. Second, Warburg's lifelong pain has something to do with his inability, or perhaps his refusal, to choose one side or the other. Professionally, he was an observer and decoder of images. But what of the culture of the observed? There is no question of any identification with a sentimental idea of a noble savage. Yet the objectification of the primitive observed is a position that remains unacceptable for Warburg. The suffering and greatness of his career and person lie in the failure, or refusal, to draw the line.

These concerns inform a crucial and disturbing passage in the opening entry of the 1923 lecture notes which Warburg marked, in the margin, as having been written while "under opium." Warburg called this first section of the notes "The Problem" and began it with the question "Why did I go there? What enticed me?" He notes his impatience with the empty civilization of the American Northeast, his encounters with the scholars at the Smithsonian, and his "will to the Romantic." He then stresses his dissatisfaction with the "aestheticizing history of art" and the "formal consideration of the image" in which he had been trained. (Warburg rejects two fin-de-siècle formalisms: those of art historical as well as religious, ritual practice.) Recalling his return to Hamburg in the summer of 1896, he remarks (in the passage I have already cited) that he had not yet realized how important his identification of an organic and indestructible primitive culture would be for his studies of the Florentine Renaissance and the Reformation.[39]

The passage proceeds to mention Warburg's discovery of Nordenskjöld's work on the cliff dwellings and then slips into the following associations, whose nonsequiturs may be at least partially explained by the already mentioned margin note, "under opium":

> To my question as to whether one might visit these cliff dwellings came the answer that, since it was already the end of November, I would be faced with overcoming the severe difficulties of winter. Also because I had been in military service, which I had acquitted with great zeal, but finally with failure, since I was discharged only as a noncommissioned officer. I had come to know anti-Semitism in its creeping form [*in seiner schleichenden Form*] as a fundamental danger for Germany, to which I might add that I have never felt myself to possess the quality of a really good reserve officer, but that those others—who advanced on the ground of their proper religion—were even worse and above all, that really able German Jews were driven out of the army as officers, something that 1914 avenged quite bloodily. A couple of thousand more Jewish officers and we might perhaps have won the slaughter of the Marne.[40]

The fundamental cultural irrationality of anti-Semitism seems here to displace the irrational elements of primitive religion, including Judaism, and shift the position of the Jew to one of support for the modern war machine—a manifestation of modernization in which Warburg at other times has no interest. Anti-Semitism as the ultimate cultural danger—for *Germany*, qua civilization—is represented as a "creeping form": a reference to the serpent, if also to the dangers of the cultural and social applications of form (i.e., aestheticism) itself.

The Sassetti and Luther Paradigms

Is Warburg's 1923 recollection that the notion of the "primitive" he gathered from the journey to the Hopi informed an idea of recurrent primitivism apparent in the Florentine Renaissance and the German Reformation borne out by his own major studies of these cultural universes? In question are his two essays on the art patron Francesco Sassetti written in 1902 and 1907 and one on pagan wisdom in the cultural context of Martin Luther, completed in late 1919.[41]

Warburg clearly saw his family and himself reflected in the life of Francesco Sassetti (1421–90), Florentine merchant and "general manager" of the Medici bank.[42] The cultural problem illustrated in his life is that of transition, in this case from the medieval world to the early modern one. Although Sassetti exemplified the Florentine humanist, Warburg was interested in showing the continuities of medieval culture: business and banking existed in close negotiation with the church, religion, and art. Like Warburg, Sassetti liked mottoes, and Warburg pointed out that he characterized his own person by two contradictory ones: the arrogant *à mon pouvoir* (to my power) and the compensatory *mitia fata mihi* (may the fates be gentle with me).[43] We might recall Warburg's own contradictory mottoes: "Athens wants precisely to be reconquered anew from Alexandria" and "the kinship of Athens and Oraibi." In the Sassetti studies, Florence, as cultural universe, mediates between, on one side, the "primitive," church-centered culture of the Middle Ages, and, on the other, the rationalizing ideals of the new Athens (or, more relevant to the Sassetti chapel's imagery, the new Rome) and the image of a secularized Renaissance—a new paganism, perhaps.

The origins of the Sassetti chapel in the church of Santa Trinità lie in questions of ecclesiastical politics. The Sassetti family had been patrons of the Dominican church of Santa Maria Novella. Sassetti engaged the painter Ghirlandaio, who had worked in Santa Maria Novella, to paint the frescoes for his tomb but asked that the scenes represent a life of Saint Francis, Francesco's patron saint. The prospect of representing the life of the founder of a rival order upset the administrators of Santa Maria, and they rejected the commission, forcing Sassetti to relocate to Santa Trinità. This is the first level of the "primitivism" as identified by Warburg: medieval-style religious disputes remained important, he showed, in the late Quattrocento, which Burckhardt and others had described as well on the way to secularization.

The second dimension of this "primitivism" has to do with the iconography of Ghirlandaio's nativity scene, the centerpiece of the altar and hence of the chapel itself. In the closing lines of the 1902 essay, Warburg suggests that Ghirlandaio's style has to do with the growing taste for Flemish art in the circle of Lorenzo de' Medici. He only hints at this affinity and says that the question of the taste for Flemish art is for another study.[44] As Eve Borsook and Johannes Offerhaus point out, the "general arrangement of the figures and especially the portrait-like rendering of the shepherd acknowledges Ghirlandaio's study of Hugo van der Goes' Portinari altarpiece which reached Florence in May 1483."[45] Warburg treated this relationship and the question of the influence of Flemish art on Florentine painters and patrons in other essays. In Gombrich's words, "Here was another aspect of that paradox which did not seem to square with the idea of Florence as an island of modernity in a Europe plunged into darkness."[46] As late as January 1929, in his lecture at the Hertziana in Rome, "Journey of Discovery to the Sources of European Enthusiasm," Warburg used the Ghirlandaio–van der Goes relationship as a central example.[47]

Warburg's long study of the German Reformation, based on a lecture in Berlin and documented through prints and books, was published in 1920. It dates from a much darker period of his life, that of his descent into mental illness. A massive essay, whose contents I do not attempt to summarize, it contains, as an epigraph to the opening section, the quotation from Goethe's *Faust,* Part 2 which generated his Athens-Oraibi motto, as well as, in a section already quoted, the metaphor of Athens's recurrent recapitulation to Alexandria.[48] The subtitle Warburg proposes in the opening paragraph is "The Renaissance of Demoniac Antiquity in the Period of the German Reformation."[49] Winckelmann and his successors, Warburg argues, had initiated a German classicism based on antiquity's Olympian side; the demoniac side has been overlooked.[50] In the Reformation period, astrology exists as the "uniformly primitive tool" (*einheitlich primitives Gerät*), as the march of an epoch in which "logic and magic, like trope and metaphor (following the words of Jean Paul) 'blossom from a graft on a single stem.'" The specific historicity in Warburg's presentation is not compromised by his immediate assertion that this very polarity is timeless (*zeitlos*).[51]

The essay is about cultural crisis and the cultural demons that, in the form of violence and irrationality, explode the myths of cultural progress. Written during and after the First World War, the essay implies a dialogue between contemporary cultural—and personal—crisis and a crucial historical antecedent. For this reason, as well as for the Reformation-period subject matter, the essay is akin to Walter Benjamin's study of the German baroque lamentation play, *Ursprung des deutschen Trauerspiels*, written between 1924 and 1928.[52] Warburg's main theme is the painful birth of a rational and humane cosmology, achieved perhaps only by the essay's two heroes, Luther and Dürer. The enemy of that cosmology is the irrational and dehumanizing cosmos of astrology. Benjamin's more overtly political main theme is the crisis of sovereignty and the failure of the baroque period (and, in his judgment, subsequent periods as well) to evolve a rational system of sovereignty (the political form of cosmology). In Warburg's analysis of culture and

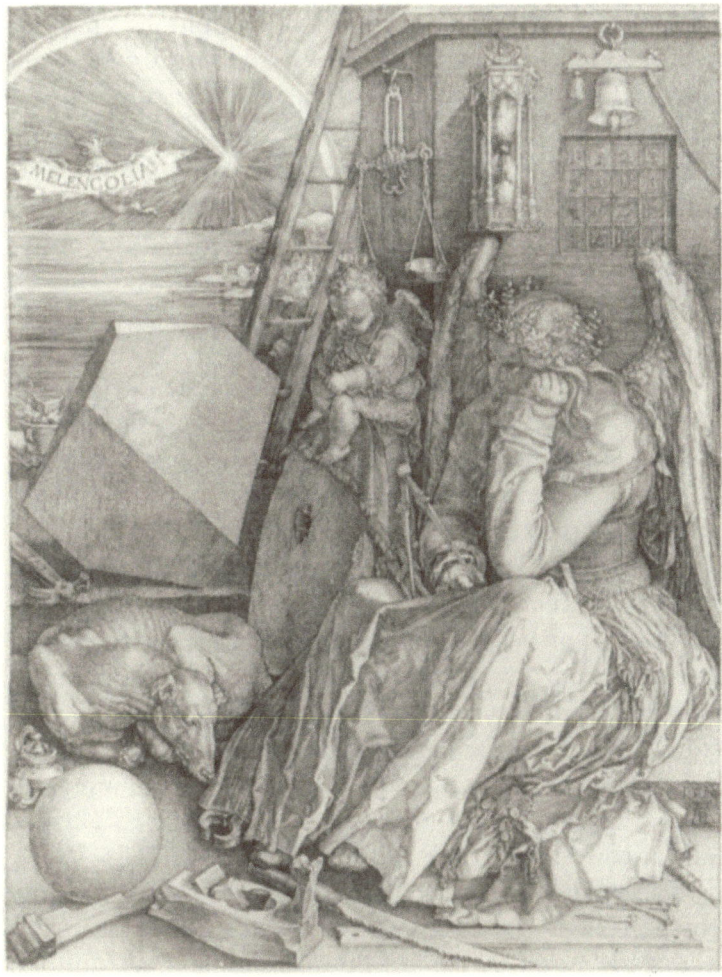

Fig. 37. Albrecht Dürer, "Melencolia I" (1514). Photo: Warburg Institute.

ABY WARBURG'S KREUZLINGEN LECTURE

personality and in Benjamin's of politics and its representations (including ritual drama), the condition from which Reformation culture strives to emancipate itself, with only occasional success, is that of melancholia. For Warburg, the overcoming of melancholy implies the Reformation and modernity's development of distance— *Distanz.* For Benjamin, it promises the birth of the political. Both scholars conclude their studies with a discussion of melancholia and, specifically, of its transformation as manifest in Dürer's "Melencolia" of 1514 (*Figure 37*).

Warburg compares Luther, who overcame the psychic pressures of astrology, to Melanchthon, who succumbed to them. For example, Melanchthon insisted at least until 1539 that Luther's birth year was, like his own, 1484, rather than the correct year of 1483, because astrologers had charted the later year as a year of planetary conjunction and hence of a new epoch in Western religion.[53] Warburg identifies the "birthday cult" of the early Reformation period as a crucial episode in "the development of modern 'homo nonsapiens.'"[54] Luther mocked the astrologers and remarked that though they had predicted a conjunction of the ugly and evil planets Saturn and Jupiter and hence a deluge (*Sündflut*) for the year 1524, they had failed to predict the peasant uprising of 1525.[55]

The image on which Warburg spends most time, and which presages the discussion of Dürer's "Melencolia," is that of the monk with a devil on his shoulder, as found in a woodcut of the 1492 Mainz edition of Johannes Lichtenberger's *Weissagungen*, held in the Hamburg Stadtbibliothek (*Figure 38*). In a footnote, Warburg notes that this image, as well as others of the same subject, portray the devil resting on the monk's shoulder atop the drape of his cowl, which falls "serpentlike" [*schlangenartig*] to the ground.[56] Next to the monk stands a smaller, timider second monk. Written in next to the images, in sixteenth-century plattdeutsch, are the identifications "Dyth is Martinus Luther" and "Philippus

Monach⁹ i alba cuculla �ᴣ diabol⁹ i ſcapuľ eiusretro
habenaleripipíum lõgum ad terã.cum amplis etiã brachũabñs piſcipulũ ſecũſtantem.

93

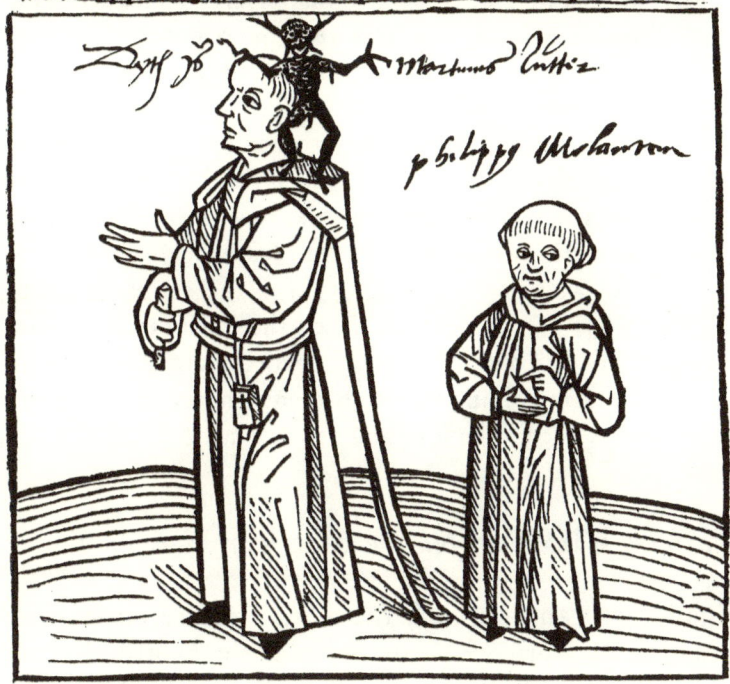

Fig. 38. Johannes Lichtenberger, *Weissagungen,* The two monks (Luther and Melanchthon). Mainz, 1492. Photo: Warburg Institute.

Melanton."[57] Luther countered with the argument that the devil in the print represented the pope.

The nobility of the image in Dürer's "Melencolia" indicates for Warburg the transformation of the demon into the representation of contemplative genius. Gombrich describes the representation as "the beginning of the struggle [for intellectual and religious emancipation]. . . . Just as Luther is still filled with the fear of the cosmic *monstra* and portents . . . so Melencolia, too, does not yet feel free from the fear of the ancient demons."[58] The passion that informs Gombrich's own conclusion merits quoting at some length:

ABY WARBURG'S KREUZLINGEN LECTURE

In the words on Dürer's "Melencolia"—which for all their recondite and learned subject-matter are so charged with suppressed emotion that they read like a poem in prose— we sense a deep feeling of kinship between the author and the work he selected for analysis. We feel that for him, too, victory is not yet. He, too, is crowned not with laurel but with nightshade, the remedy against the dreaded influence of Saturn. For when these lines were written, the issue of the struggle was in the balance. The war years had increased Warburg's excitability and the sense of doom which had settled on him. When the breakdown of Germany in 1918 had confirmed his worst fears, he no longer succeeded in holding the encroaching demons at bay. Alexandria seemed to have conquered Athens.[59]

Warburg's Texts on Native American Paganism

Finally, we can approach the actual lecture on serpent ritual of 21 April 1923, or rather a single strand in it, which contains the working out and the working through of Warburg's mature phenomenological and emotional position on paganism. I begin with the short reports and lectures he gave soon after his return to Germany in May 1896, which he then put away until the turning point of 1923.

The 1897 lectures, with slides, provided much ethnographic information and a certain amount of vicarious tourism to eager audiences. Warburg also tried, briefly, to negotiate the sale of ceremonial objects to museums in Germany. His main contact in this enterprise was Jesse Walter Fewkes of the Smithsonian. While still in New Mexico, on 5 April 1896, Warburg wrote to Fewkes and reported the progress of his itinerary. Once back in Hamburg, on 10 October 1896, he wrote again to Fewkes, reporting the interest of Professor Grünwald of the Ethnographisches Museum in Berlin in purchasing some

Moki [Hopi] kachina dolls as well as other objects. "Can
you have something excavated for us?" he asks. On 7
December he wrote again, this time from Berlin, reporting his intention to give a lecture on his journey and ask-
ing how to get in touch with the Reverend Mr. Voth. (As
this was to be a slide lecture, it is possible that he wanted
more photographs.) The final extant letter dates from 15
February 1897 and reports that the Berlin museum would
pay between two and three thousand marks for Hopi ceramics and other ceremonial objects.[60] This correspondence, in addition to showing an otherwise unrevealed
entrepreneurial side to Warburg's adventure, shows as
well his short-term distance from the sacred aura, to say
nothing of the demonology, of the culture to which he
had just been introduced.

The three lectures he gave confirm this distance. On
21 January 1897 he spoke to the Hamburg Photographic
Society. He began with a historical sketch of the southwest region and a summary of the ethnographic work of
Adolf Bandelier, Frank Hamilton Cushing, Washington
Matthews, and Matilda Coxe Stevenson. He introduced
his slides with the qualification that they represented "un
coin de la nature vu par un Kodak" (a corner of nature
seen through a Kodak).[61] On 10 February 1897 he spoke
to the American Club of Hamburg, introducing his photographs [Augenblicksbilder: literally, momentary im-
ages] "from the life of the Pueblo Indians." He showed
about fifty slides. This talk contained much more descriptive ethnography and historical summary than the
first one had. He discussed, for example, a Hopi kachina
dance he had observed in Oraibi on 1 May 1896, just
before he left the region. He described the dancers as
"neither gods . . . nor priests, . . . [but] mediums."[62]

On 16 March 1897 he spoke to the Free Photographic
Union of Berlin (Freie photographische Vereinigung), and
his lecture title, "Images from the Life of the Pueblo Indians in North America," presaged the title of the 1923 lec-

ture.[63] He reflected that "what drew me, as an art historian, to visit the groups of Pueblo Indians in New Mexico and Arizona was that the conjunction of pagan religious representations and artistic activity is nowhere more recognizable than among the Pueblo Indians and that in their culture one can find rich material for the study of the question of the development of symbolic art."

Perhaps Warburg's sense of duty to return to the professional practice of art history led him to identify himself so unequivocally as an art historian. He had clearly been thinking as a cultural anthropologist and historian from the time of his departure for America. In the well known appraisal of his colleague Fritz Saxl, "Warburg was indeed the student not only of Justi and Janitschek, but also of Usener, in other words of the trend in the German historiography of religion which—like Frazer in England—strove to understand the ancient texts and the origin of Greek and Roman religion with the help of still extant paganism. It was thus as a student of Usener that he went to Santa Fe, to Albuquerque, and to the region of the Mesa Verde."[64] In sum, Warburg's short-term assimilation and representation of his experiences in the American Southwest reflect a rich descriptive ethnography but, at the same time, a certain degree of emotional as well as professional rigidity.

His return to the material in 1923 occurred in a context of pain. Although we must certainly heed Gombrich's charge neither to diagnose nor to romanticize Warburg's condition, we do have the evidence to allow two suggestions: first, that Warburg lived in agony; second, that he vented his agony and his vacillating ability to think as a scholar through an uninterrupted flow of personal diary entries.[65] Warburg always wrote, sometimes only symptomatically, sometimes with no border between a symptomatic voice and a scholarly one. There exists as well a leather volume that Warburg had apparently received in

1892, left empty, and taken with him to Kreuzlingen. On the first page he had inscribed "Gedenkbuch" (book of remembrance) and the date, 2 September 1892. On the frontispiece is inscribed "Was nicht dein ist, rühr nicht an! A. Warburg. Eigenthum" (What is not yours, do not disturb! A. Warburg. Personal property). The inscription and, apparently, all subsequent entries, written in pencil, date from 1921. This particular volume, perhaps for its bridge across time, seems to have retained a talismanic value for Warburg during the Kreuzlingen years. Above the "Gedenkbuch" inscription, he wrote "Will 1921 finally bring me the return to Hamburg?" Next to that: "No." Then, line by line: "And 1922?" "No." "And 1923?" "Disappointment." "And 1924? Back to Hamburg!"

A few entries made before the lecture bear citing. At one point in early April (probably the tenth, if the entries continued on a daily basis—but this one is undated), Warburg wrote that the clinic director Ludwig Binswanger might not be able to arrange the lecture for the twenty-first, as planned. "Such a lack of psychology!" His humor also turns on himself, and he refers in the same entry to the "Schlangenquatsch"—the serpent drivel. On the twelfth, he regains the guiding tone, referring to "the tragic symbol of the serpent." On the thirteenth, he records that he has asked Fritz Saxl to bring to him Lessing's *Laocoon*. Finally, in the entry of 20 April 1923, Warburg wrote that the lecture, scheduled once again for the next day, was completed. In the entry of the following evening, he wrote, "Lecture on the journey to the Pueblos took place and was a brilliant success."

The poetic momentum of the actual lecture makes it clear that the personal and scholarly resolution it marks resides not in the redemption of rationality over primitivism but in the rejection of such historical linearity and its attendant psychic and scholarly pressures altogether. The title must be taken seriously; in introducing "Images from the Region of the Pueblo Indians of North America," Warburg is, literally, showing pictures, but he is also implying a way of looking at culture and history. It is the same principle Walter Benjamin later called the "dialectical image." In question is a Platonic dialectic rather than a Hegelian one: images from history as records of cultural predicaments speak to one another, and the eyes and voice of the historian present the points of contact. Distance in space and time still separates epochs, but the images placed in dialogue overcome that distance just enough to posit associations that burst the myth of a grand, linear historical narrative with premeasured increments of cultural and temporal distance. Thus Warburg begins with ethnography and ends with observations on the culture of Uncle Sam and the telephone.

The lecture's opening pages were omitted from the version published in 1939 by the Warburg Institute. After apologies for the tenuousness of his own reconstructed memories and his linguistic limitations as far as Native American culture is concerned, Warburg states the question "In what ways can we perceive essential character traits of primitive pagan humanity?" Whereas in the 1897 lectures he had used the phrase "What interested me as an art historian," here he says, "What interested me as a cultural historian was that in the midst of a country that had made technological culture into an admirable precision weapon in the hands of intellectual man, an enclave of primitive pagan humanity was able to maintain itself." This culture appears as a "symptom of a completely backward humanity." In an early manuscript version of this sentence, there appears the additional phrase—which was struck out and which therefore never appeared in a published version—"incapable of life, crippled by a dark superstition." Although such condemnation of the demoniac aspects of primitive culture

MICHAEL P. STEINBERG

speaks to Warburg's fears ("the poisonous serpent," he
states, "belongs in the fire"), his own editorial changes
reveal how the maturations of his argument, in the actual
process of preparing the lecture, inflected his growing
ambivalence toward "primitive" ritualistic practice.[66]

Warburg's shifting paradigm seems to achieve full realization in the following paragraph, unpublished until
the German edition of 1988: "This synchrony
[*Nebeneinander*] of fantastic magic and sober purposiveness appears as the symptom of a cleavage; for the Indian
this is not schizoid but, rather, a liberating experience of
the boundless communicability between man and environment."[67] The seminal term here is *Nebeneinander*, literally, "next to one another." It is Lessing's term, from
Laocoon, and represents his argument that the visual arts
are perceived in terms of synchronic individual images, as
opposed to other forms, including words, where the re-
ceptive experience is diachronic, or *Nacheinander*. This
synchrony dictates the relative moderation of visual imagery: the sigh in the sculpture of the dying Laocoon as
opposed to the screams described by Virgil. As we know,
Warburg had requested a copy of *Laocoon* weeks before
the lecture, after the extant notes had been completed.
The principle of *Nebeneinander* informs and transforms
the actual lecture. For Warburg, it is a principle of re-
deeming ambivalence, through which paganism and rationality are allowed never to be reconciled but to exist in
dialogue nonetheless.

The first mention of the serpent symbol follows this
new principle of ambivalence. In the presymbolic phase,
the serpent *is* lightning: it is danger, but it is also rain and
corn. The serpent is the "uncanny animal" (*das unheim-
liche Tier*); its symbology emanates, suggests Warburg in
a universalist speculation, from the fact that "contemplation of the sky is the grace and curse of humanity." Finally, "the social provision of food is schizoid: magic and
technology work together." The serpent poses the ques-

tion "To what extent does this pagan worldview, as it persists among the Indians, give us a yardstick for the development from primitive paganism, through the paganism of classical antiquity, to modern man?"

Warburg now describes these convergences as the "synchrony [*Nebeneinander*] of logical civilization and fantastic, magical causation." This is a point of argumentative as well as lyric transition in Warburg's argument, where the essay leaves behind the traces of thirty years of notes. The synchrony, or at least the ambiguity, of magic and technology stand in for the ambiguity of paganism and rationality. This ambiguity holds within an individual cultural context (the Hopi, Sassetti's Florence, Luther's Reformation) as well as comparatively. A temporal, transitional dimension does remain, however, because Warburg still adheres to a paradigm of historical modernization and rationalization in a Weberian sense. Here he describes the transition as proceeding from *Greifen* to *Begriff*, from literality ("grasping") to conceptualization ("concept"), terms he returned to in a 1924 essay on symbolism.[68] The term and principle of *Nebeneinander* stuck to Warburg as well; in his Hamburg seminar of 1927–28, he reinvoked the parallel of van der Goes and Ghirlandaio, which he had addressed in the Sassetti essays, and described their stylistic convergence as a moment of cultural "*Nebeneinander*."[69]

The immediate rhetorical effect of the principle of *Nebeneinander* is to shorten the distance between pagan and rational culture. Following Frank Hamilton Cushing, Warburg mentions the Indian belief in animal ancestry and describes clan nomenclature as "a Darwinism of mythical elective affinity which determines the lives of these so-called primitive people."[70] We have seen the invocations of Lessing and Goethe; the presence of Nietzsche returns as well. Warburg had described his urge to travel to the Southwest as "the will to the Romantic"; now, in a short section comparing the kachina dance to ancient tragedy, he is in the realm of *The Birth of Tragedy*. He compares the accompanying dances to the tragic chorus.[71] The chorus is the anthropomorphic symbol for the cycles of nature. Thus dance and drama fulfill a function parallel to pictorial representation and operate at a far distance from the process of human sacrifice evident in Mexican cults, which Warburg does indeed describe as lunatic.

The paradigm of a borderline pagan-rational practice established, Warburg describes the serpent ritual of Walpi, which he himself did not witness. Again, there is no question of sacrificing the sacred animal, in contrast to the dance of the Maenads in the orgiastic cult of Dionysius. Warburg comments: "The deliverance from blood sacrifice as the innermost ideal of purification pervades the history of religious evolution from east to west. The serpent shares in this process of religious sublimation." In this judgment, then, the conventional paradigm of Athens and Oraibi is reversed. The symbol of the serpent travels the course of the history of religion, from the symbol of evil of the Old Testament's Babylonian primal serpent Tiamat and Moses' order to the Hebrews in the desert to cure snakebite by honoring a serpent image; to the Greek subterranean monster, as in the Laocoon story; to the New Testament story of Paul against the vipers of Malta. The bibilical serpent, from the Garden of Eden onward, represents the root of evil, sin, and satanic power. Similarly, the death of Laocoon represents the revenge of demons, "without justice and without hope of redemption. That is the hopeless, tragic pessimism of antiquity." This is, however, not the identity of the serpent of Walpi, and Warburg locates the point of transition in the cult of Asclepius: "Asclepius, the ancient god of healing, carries a serpent coiling around his healing staff as a symbol. His features are the features carried by the world savior in the plastic art of antiquity."[72]

In a highly emotional passage, Warburg shows how

early images of Asclepius identify him with the serpent itself: "It is he himself who winds around his staff." The serpent is the site of violence and regeneration combined: "The snake also reveals by its own ability to cast off its slough, slipping, as it were, out of its own mortal remains, how a body can leave its skin and continue to live." The serpent is Warburg.

The serpent is the site of the uncanny and the ambiguous. It is transmitted through Western culture, through the Hebrew and Christian Bibles and Greek mythology into the syncretism of medieval and early modern manifestations through the rationalizations of modernity. The road to enlightenment deepens the uncanny and the ambiguous. Warburg tells of an image of Laocoon that he had spotted in a church in Lüdingworth, near Hamburg—close to home. In this image, Laocoon is redeemed by Asclepius. What does this happy end represent? Is it the force of enlightenment? Or is it the enlightened claim to truth which is, in truth, an act of censorship, the suppression in narrative and representation of the violence of the world? Must the visual image itself be reclaimed from the censorship of Lessing, restored from the claim of sophrosyne to the shock of Virgil's words?

The conclusions to Warburg's foray into comparative ethnography offer dialectical imagery of Hopi America and the modernized landscape of United States expansion. Modern America has no need, Warburg suggests, for the serpent as an explanation of lightning. The modern American does not worship the serpent; he kills it. Warburg then introduces a coda on the question of pagan culture versus rationalized, disenchanted modernity. He recalls the episode with the schoolchildren at Keams Canyon as the manifestation of empirical cultural flux and normative cultural ambivalence. The education provided to these children by the Indian School Service will speed this process of acculturation and modernization. Invoking Plato, he asserts, "Children stand before a cave. To

MICHAEL P. STEINBERG

lift them up to the light is the task not only of American schools but of humanity in general." But, he warns—with the help of a photograph of a Gilded Age gentleman strolling beneath a power line—the conquerer of the cult of the serpent is "Uncle Sam in his stovepipe hat, strolling in his pride past a neoclassical rotunda. Above his top hat runs an electric wire. In this copper serpent of Edison's, he has wrested lightning from nature." Warburg's concluding tones are unambiguous:

> The American of today is no longer afraid of the rattlesnake. He kills it; in any case he does not worship it. It now faces extermination. The lightning imprisoned in wire—captured electricity—has produced a culture with no use for paganism. What has replaced it? Natural forces are no longer seen in anthropomorphic or biomorphic guise, but rather as infinite waves obedient to the human touch. With these waves, the culture of the machine age destroys what the natural sciences, born of myth, so arduously achieved: the space for devotion, which evolved in turn into the space required for reflection.
>
> The modern Prometheus and the modern Icarus, Franklin and the Wright brothers, who invented the dirigible airplane, are precisely those ominous destroyers of the sense of distance, who threaten to lead the planet back into chaos.
>
> Telegram and telephone destroy the cosmos. Mythical and symbolic thinking strive to form spiritual bonds between humanity and the surrounding world, shaping distance into the space required for devotion and reflection: the distance undone by the instantaneous electric connection.

Warburg thus ends his lecture with an expression of sympathy for an auratic, mythical past as opposed to the disenchantment of rationalized modernity. Yet crucial to the movement of his argument is his retention of the notion of distance. Warburg's growing sympathy with a mythical or magical cosmology thus has nothing whatsoever to do with the nostalgia for an undiffentiated community characteristic of a Stefan George or a Heidegger. If, during the course of most of his work to this point, Warburg had defined distance as the effortful creation of rationality and modernity, won by Luther and the Reformation from the magic of pre-Renaissance religious practice, he now sees distance as a legacy of an auratic past that is compromised by modern technology. Distance is the dignity of the subject and is, as such, the product of difficult cultural work, at no time a given, and in no way a presumable privilege of the modern world.

The Critique of Aestheticism

In his persona as a "German scientist" (as he was identified on his letter of introduction from the Department of the Interior), Warburg observed the spread of the white American empire and the closing of the western frontier from the standpoint of a German citizen born on the eve of Prussian supremacy and the *Gründerzeit* of the German Empire. Through this lens, primitive cultures as well as ancient ones gathered new relevance. Despite his German posture, Warburg's sympathy was for the subjected, for the Pueblo Indian whose imagery, culture, and commerce were being replaced by those—literally, in the images he stressed—of Uncle Sam. Surely the parallel of the wandering American Indian minority and its "primitive" traditions (remember that Warburg used the quotation marks) to that of the Jews in imperial Germany occurred to him. The American Indians and the German Jews faced similar predicaments of assimilation and orthodoxy.

But to neither the German Jewish predicament nor the American Indian did Warburg's attitude evince sentimentality. In his lecture of 16 March 1897, Warburg

warned against the sentimental and romantic image of
the American Indian which had informed German imagi-
nations. In both cases, the modern incarnation of the pagan or the "primitive" represented chaos and danger. The
problem was that the obvious alternative—the rejection
of the primitive, the faith in rationality and sophrosyne—
appeared itself as a romantic alternative, an aesthetic
ideal that faded as society or the individual reached for it.

In the 1923 lecture notes, Warburg described his im-
pulse to travel to the West in terms of the wish to escape
the "aestheticizing art history" of his training. His mature treatment of cultural representation remains consis-
tent with this position. The interpretation of images—
and the dynamic images of ceremonial dances—require
the recognition of cultural violence, of demons. These
forces cannot be aestheticized; on the contrary, the image
of Laocoon proves that aesthetic form can have only limited power over cultural violence. In this respect, the aesthetic analysis of Warburg is anti-aestheticist; it stands
militantly on the critical side of European intellectual
life, next to Benjamin, and opposite, ultimately, the fas-
cist energies that proceed according to the
aestheticization of politics.

Warburg's 1923 Kreuzlingen lecture, replete with its
potential for self-conscious theatricality, represents an
intellectual as well as a personal and therapeutic moment
of achievement. Clearly, for Warburg, the two categories
had to exist together. There is no synthesis here: he did
not reconcile the primitive and the modern, the chaotic
and the rational, certainly not the formless (which has
nothing to do with the "primitive" anyway) and the
formed. But through the act of scholarship and criticism,
he placed the two in front of his eyes and gained perspective on their ambivalence and ambiguity in relation to
each other. Insofar as these elements were part of himself,
he was able to look at himself. Of the varied relationships
between a late-nineteenth-century German "self" and a

primitive "other," the sentimental Orientalism of Karl May is at one extreme, where the other has no subjectivity and the self reimposes its preexisting ideologies. Although it seems inappropriate to describe Aby Warburg's intellectual style according to any kind of extreme, it seems certain that his critical and cultural passion derived from a lifelong refusal to delineate boundaries between self and other, personal and cultural—and this during a period when the abnegation of the ideology of cultural identity was not a popular intellectual alternative.

The last period of Warburg's life, from his return to Hamburg in 1924 to his death in October 1929, called for the refocusing of his social and cultural paradigms. As his health returned, he paid more attention to the institutional growth of the Warburg Library in Hamburg. The library enjoyed a productive relationship with the newly founded University of Hamburg and strove as well to establish international contacts. In this context, Warburg sought to resume and retain contacts with American institutions in order to revive his work in comparative ethnology.

"On the whole I feel much better whenever American friends visit" (*Überhaupt, wenn Amerikanische Freunde kommen, geht es mir gleich besser*), wrote Warburg to Paul J. Sachs in October 1926. Sachs was the associate director of the William Hayes Fogg Museum at Harvard University from 1923 until 1948. As the son of Louisa Goldman and Samuel Sachs, he had abandoned banking for art in a manner that attracted Warburg's sympathy. They corresponded enthusiastically between 1925 and 1928.[73]

In the fall of 1927, Warburg wrote a memorandum to his brothers emphasizing the importance of these American contacts as well as the continuing centrality of his work on the Hopi to his evolving scholarship. Most specifically, he was determined to make a second American journey, and for this he needed his brothers' financing.[74]

He singles out Paul Sachs in Cambridge and also Franz
Boas and his student Gladys Reichard at Columbia University. Reichard had just visited him in Hamburg. He
also mentions "Washington," by which he presumably
means the Smithsonian. (James Mooney had died in
1921, and Warburg does not seem to have had contact
with his successors.) His goal is to form an "organic connection" between the Warburg Library and these institutions, with a series of seminars devoted to the theme of
"the tradition of antiquity for modern cultures as a life
problem." As for his own role, Warburg envisioned a
three-month trip for early 1928, during which he would
lecture at the Fogg on "pagan-ancient tradition in the
mirror of European art" and at Columbia on "the significance of ethnologic American research for the fundamental principles of cultural studies." He had already corresponded with Boas about this latter initiative. On this
American journey, he says, he will no longer have the energy for a side trip (*ein Abstecher*) to Arizona and New
Mexico. "I must admit," he says, "I am a very bad trav-
eler." The return to America, he suggests, will close a
circle defining his life's work:

> When I look back on my life's journey, it appears to me
> that my function has been to serve the watersheds
> [*Wetterscheide*] of culture as a seismograph of souls. Pos-
> ited from my very birth in the middle ground between Ori-
> ent and Occident, driven by the force of elective affinity to
> Italy, where in the fifteenth century the confluence of pa-
> gan antiquity and Christian Renaissance caused an entirely
> new cultural persona to emerge, I was also driven to travel
> to America in the service of extrapersonal causes, in order
> to experience life there in its polar tension between pagan,
> instinctual forces of nature and organized intelligence.

On 28 December 1927, Warburg wrote to Paul Sachs
about his projected return to America, stating that his

chief goal was to build bridges between the young and old of the American academic world and those of the old and new Europe. He also asked Sachs to help persuade "my loving and caring brothers" (Paul and Felix in New York) of the advisability of the trip: "I would then have the chance once again to see America, which I have loved with unyielding force for thirty-three years."[75]

Warburg's second American journey never materialized. He did, however, return to Italy in 1929 for a last extended visit. His timing proved savagely ironic. Having worked through the presence of his own demons, he witnessed the return of the demoniac to European culture. The story is told by Arnaldo Momigliano:

> Gertrud Bing, the Director of the Warburg Institute, used to tell with great gusto a story that apparently has not found its way into the biography of Aby Warburg by Ernst Gombrich. Bing happened to be in Rome with Warburg, the founder and patron saint of the Warburg Institute, on that day, February 11, 1929, on which Mussolini and the Pope proclaimed the reconciliation between Italy and the Catholic Church and signed a concordat, the first bilateral agreement to be reached between post-Risorgimento Italy and the Church of Rome. There were in Rome tremendous popular demonstrations, whether orchestrated from above or from below. Mussolini became overnight the "man of providence," and in such an inconvenient position he remained for many years. Circulation in the streets of Rome was not very easy on that day, and it so happened that Warburg disappeared from the sight of his companions. They anxiously waited for him back in the Hotel Eden, but there was no sign of him for dinner. Bing and the others even telephoned the police. But Warburg reappeared in the hotel before midnight, and when he was reproached he soberly replied something like this in his picturesque German: "You know that throughout my life I have been interested in the revival of paganism and pagan festivals. Today

I had the chance of my life to be present at the repaganization of Rome, and you complain that I remained
to watch it."[76]

Warburg apparently witnessed the return of pagan
demons with a certain remove and a tone that reflected
his own inner sophrosyne. But even this position, bal-
anced and altogether charming as it is, is not to be ro-
manticized. How are we to read Warburg's tone: as comic
distance or as savage irony? Does the secure sense of distance Warburg shows in representing Italian fascism as a
pagan comedy appear as a failure or as a success of his
long-germinating method of negotiating the dangerous
realities of cultural demons? The heritage of distance, of
critique and subjectivity, is the heritage defeated by the
repaganization borne by European fascism, and we can
only guess whether Warburg's comic representation
meant for him a strategy of avoidance, an unspoken pro-
gram for victory, or a tragic realization of defeat.
Mussolini's victories were succeeded by Hitler's. In late
1933, four years after Warburg's death, the Warburg library and its method were removed from Hamburg to
London and thus extracted from a context where
Denkraum—the space for reflection—had been destroyed.

NOTES

1. The alliance had begun six months earlier with the marriage of Felix Warburg to Frieda Schiff, daughter of Kuhn-Loeb senior partner Jacob Schiff. Nina Loeb was in fact Frieda Schiff's maternal aunt, which made Paul the uncle of his brother. See David Farrer, *The Warburgs: The Story of a Family* . (New York: 1975).

2. Claudia Naber, "Pompeji in Neu-Mexico: Aby Warburgs amerikanische Reise," *Freibeuter* 38 (1988): 89.

3. E. H. Gombrich, *Aby Warburg: An Intellectual Biography* (1970; Chicago, 1986). Gombrich's translation of "der Wille zum Romantischen" is, curiously, "an urge towards the Romantic" (p. 88). Warburg's language clearly contains a Nietzsche parody which reinforces a certain wry distance from his youthful attitudes.

4. Gombrich, p. 89.

5. See Naber, pp. 90–91.

6. James Mooney, *The Ghost Dance Religion and the Sioux Outbreak of 1890*, ed. Anthony F. C. Wallace (Chicago, 1965), p. 1.

7. Anthony F. C. Wallace, introduction to Mooney, p. ix.

8. Naber, pp. 88–97.

9. See Naber, pp. 89, 96.

10. See Naber, pp. 90–91.

11. 1923 lecture notes, Warburg Archive, Warburg Institute, London.

12. Naber, p. 91.

13. See Naber, p. 94.

14. This material is in file box no. 140, marked "Americana," Warburg Archive.

15. 1923 lecture notes.

16. For a bibliography of Voth's writings as well as other information, see Peter M. Whiteley, *Deliberate Acts: Changing Hopi Culture through the Oraibi Split* (Tucson, 1988). Voth's photographs, as well as other materials, are in the Mennonite Library and Archives, Bethel College, North Newton, Kansas. Whiteley argues, with considerable evidence, that Voth was reviled among the Hopi for "subjection of Hopi religion to open scrutiny [which] ran directly counter to Hopi practice" (p. 84). Whiteley quotes the Mennonite historian Alfred Siemens as follows: "The first Mennonite missionary to the Hopi, H. R. Voth, was an aggressive evangelist and anthropologist. He gathered many Hopi artifacts, made intensive study of their customs, vocabulary, and religion, and wrote carefully and voluminously about them. But he, as had the Catholic fathers before him, also antagonized them. The present missionaries feel they are still the objects of a resentment that was aroused by pioneer missionaries" (p. 85). Whiteley also cites Voth's daughter's description of him (in a 1982 interview) as "a harsh man, definitely not gemütlich." Whiteley writes nevertheless that "Voth made some friends in Oraibi. He was clearly in sympathy with some Hostile [i.e., antiassimilationist] views and occasionally served as intermediary with government agents. As the only resident white who could speak Hopi fluently, he was trusted by some to interpret government policies" (p. 85). This is significant in the light of Warburg's 1923 recollection: "Through years of contact with the Indians he won their trust, and he paid as little heed as possible to his own missionary tasks. He studied the Indians, bought up their products, and developed a hefty business

MICHAEL P. STEINBERG

in the trading of these objects. As a result of the extraordinary measure of confidence he enjoyed, it was possible to photograph them during their dances, something that their fear of being photographed would otherwise never have allowed." Aby Warburg, "Notizen zum Kreuzlinger Vortrag" [1923], Warburg Archive. Warburg does not seem to have felt Hopi hostility to Voth, or, for that matter, to himself.

17. 1923 lecture notes.

18. Warburg wrote his version of the story onto a sheet of Indian School Service stationery provided by the Keams Canyon schoolteacher, F. Neel. Neel was apparently interested in Warburg's work and wrote to him about this 24 April exercise in November 1896 (Warburg Archive).

19. 1923 lecture notes.

20. Cited in A. M. Meyer, "Aby Warburg in His Early Correspondence," *American Scholar* 57 (Summer 1988): 450.

21. Gombrich, p. 215.

22. George L. Mosse, *Germans and Jews beyond Judaism* (Bloomington, 1985), p. 52.

23. Gombrich, p. 214.

24. For a discussion of Binswanger, Heidegger, and the relation of phenomenology to psychoanalysis, see Gerald N. Izenberg, *The Existentialist Critique of Freud: The Crisis of Autonomy* (Princeton, N.J., 1976).

25. See Ludwig Binswanger, *Henrik Ibsen und das Problem der Selbstrealisation in der Kunst* (Heidelberg, 1949); Paul de Man, *Blindness and Insight* (Minneapolis, 1983), pp. 36–50.

26. De Man, pp. 39–40.

27. The quotation, from the "Wahn monologue" in Act 3 of *Die Meistersinger von Nürnberg*, translates as "Now let's see how Hans Sachs will be able to mold the irrational into a noble work." I might add here that it would be impertinent of me to reproach Gombrich and Mosse for their "fortress rationality" reading of Warburg. Their firsthand experience of European fascism perhaps led them to abjure negotiation with cultural demons by adopting this strict posture. It is their faith in the epistemological soundness of the posture which distances them, in my view, from Warburg.

28. My paraphrase is taken from the account in Max's privately published memoir "Dieser Vertrag war wohl der leichtsinnigste meines Lebens," in Max Warburg, *Aus meinen Aufzeichnungen* (1952). Gombrich (p. 22) quotes and translates Max's remarks of 5 December 1929 as follows: "When he was thirteen, Aby made me an offer of his birthright ("sein Erstgeborenenrecht"). . . . It was not a pottage of lentils, however, which he demanded, but a promise that I would always buy him all the books he wanted. After a very brief pause for reflection, I consented. I told myself that when I was in the business I could, after all, always find the money to pay for the works of Schiller, Goethe, Lessing, and perhaps also Klopstock, and so, unsuspecting, I gave him what I must now admit was a very large blank cheque."

29. Meyer, p. 452.

30. Meyer, p. 445.

31. Lecture notes, 16 March 1923, Warburg Archive.

32. Lecture notes, 16 March 1923; see also Gombrich, pp. 19–20.

33. Gombrich, pp. 23–24.

34. Meyer, p. 447.

35. Meyer, p. 452.

36. Meyer, p. 451.

37. Meyer, pp. 451–52.

38. See Dieter Wuttke's appendix on the distribution of materials in the Warburg Archive, "Abteilung B: Archivmaterial," in *Aby M. Warburg: Ausgewählte Schriften und Würdigungen*, ed. Wuttke (Baden-Baden, 1980), p. 585.

39. 1923 lecture notes.

40. 1923 lecture notes.

41. Aby Warburg, "Bildniskunst und florentinisches Bürgertum" (1902); "Francesco Sassettis letztwillige Verfügung" (1907), and "Heidnisch-antike Weissagung in Wort und Bild zu Luthers Zeiten" (1920), all in Wuttke, pp. 103–24, 137–64, and 199–304, respectively.

42. The anachronistic title is Eve Borsook's; see Borsook and Johannes Offerhaus, *Francesco Sassetti and Ghirlandaio at Santa Trinita, Florence: History and Legend in a Renaissance Chapel* (Doornspijk, 1981).

43. See Gombrich, p. 174.

44. "Bildniskunst," in Wuttke, p. 25.

45. Borsook and Offerhaus, p. 34.

46. Gombrich, p. 136; see also pp. 165, 175, 178. Presumably, Gombrich's point is that Flanders was, for Warburg, also modern. Perhaps the inverse was true: that, for Warburg, Florence was still primitive.

47. See Gombrich, pp. 271–72.

48. Wuttke, p. 201.

49. Wuttke, p. 201.

50. Wuttke, p. 202.

51. Wuttke, p. 203.

52. Benjamin knew Warburg's essay when he wrote the *Ursprung*. He also knew the subsequent work of Erwin Panofsky and Fritz Saxl, *Dürers 'Melencolia I': Eine quellen- und typengeschichtliche Untersuchung* (Leipzig and Berlin, 1923). As is well known, Benjamin submitted the work as his *Habilitationsschrift* at the University of Frankfurt in 1925, and it was rejected. He published it in book form in 1928, at which point Warburg acquired a copy and gave it to Saxl. I owe this last information to J. B. Trapp.

53. Wuttke, pp. 214–15.

54. Wuttke, p. 218.

55. Wuttke, pp. 231–32.

56. Wuttke, p. 237. The serpentine flow of the garment in the image is a function of Warburg's viewing. Its referents are just as likely to be the Hopi snakes as the more relevant antecedent of Lucifer.

57. Wuttke, p. 238.

58. Gombrich, p. 213.

59. Gombrich, p. 215.

60. The four letters are written in German (Fewkes had studied in Leipzig). I read copies of them in the Warburg Archive. The originals are held by the Smithsonian. The Museum für Völkerkunde in Hamburg holds 74 objects, from an original number of 136, which Warburg collected himself; another 19 are in Dresden; and 43 were destroyed by fire—this according to Wuttke, pp. 583–84. Warburg also corresponded, between January and March 1905, with Emil Bibo of the Cubero Trading Company, which specialized in Acoma pottery. Bibo sent Warburg films of matachin dances as well as still photographs. In one of Bibo's letters, he mentions his brother, Solomon, by this time residing in San Francisco. This is a figure of considerable interest. A German Jew, Solomon Bibo arrived in Santa Fe in 1869, founded the trad-

MICHAEL P. STEINBERG

ing company atop the Acoma mesa in 1882, married an Acoma woman, and in 1885 became the only non-Indian to be elected governor of Acoma. The United States authorities, and finally the Acoma themselves, grew suspicious of Bibo's motives, and he ultimately fled to California. One wonders what Warburg's reaction might have been to this German Jewish predecessor in the Southwest. See Gordon Bronitsky, "Solomon Bibo," *New Mexico* 68:8 (August 1990): 98–102. Emil Bibo's letters are in file box no. 140, marked "Americana," Warburg Archive.

61. Warburg, "Bericht für die photographische Gesellschaft: Eine Reise durch das Gebiet der Pueblo Indianer in Nordamerika," Warburg Archive. Warburg's French phrase, true to his characteristic love for mottoes, derives from Emile Zola: "J'exprimerai toute ma pensée en disant qu'un oeuvre d'art est un coin de la création vu à travers un tempérament" ("All my thinking can be described by the definition of a work of art as a corner of creation seen through a certain temperament." Zola, "M. H. Taine, artiste," in *Mes Haines* [1866], *Oeuvres complètes d'Emile Zola* [Paris, 1928], p. 176). Assuming that Warburg was aware of his source in deriving his own phrase, we might speculate about the replacement of "temperament" with "Kodak": the substitution of technology and the technical eye for sensibility.

62. Warburg Archive.

63. "Bilder aus dem Leben der Pueblo-Indianer in Nordamerika," Warburg Archive; cited by Naber, pp. 92–93; 96. This lecture was published in the *Photographische Rundschau: Zeitschrift für Freunde der Photographie*, ed. R. Neuhass, 11 Jahrgang 1897, Vereinsnachrichten 61.

64. Fritz Saxl, "Warburgs Besuch in Neu-Mexico" (1929/30–1957), in Wuttke, pp. 317–26; 318.

65. The diaries from the Kreuzlingen years are in the Warburg Archive. They were identified already by Ludwig Binswanger as strictly clinical material; Gombrich chose not to cite them and Wuttke did not catalog them.

66. Warburg's (published) words are "als Symptom eines ganz zurückgebliebenen Menschentums" (*Schlangenritual*, p. 10.) The earlier version (with the omitted words in small capitals) would have rendered the sentence as "als Symptom eines ganz zurückgebliebenen LEBENSUNFÄHIGEN Menschentums DAS EIN FINSTERER ABERGLAUBE LÄHMT" (Lecture manucript, Warburg Archive). The published German lecture text of 1988 contains additional such examples. In Warburg's description of the solo dancers accompanying the humiskachina dance at Oraibi, the phrase "extremely coarse [überaus derbe]" had at one point read as "plain indecent [direkt unanständige]" (*Schlangentritual*, p. 40 as opposed to 1938 manuscript, Warburg Archive). The following paragraph was first restored in the 1988 edition: "The simulated pantomimic animal dance is thus a cultic act of the highest devotion and self-abandon to an alien being. The masked dance of so-called primitive peoples is in its original essence a document of social piety" (*Schlangenritual*, p. 27). I have noted earlier that the "fortress rationality" position, which Warburg so clearly turns away from in the writing of the lecture, has continued to control the reception of his thinking, especially that of Gombrich. For an illuminating application of this tendency toward interpretive shifts in general among Warburg Institute scholars of several generations, see Carlo Ginzburg, "From Aby Warburg to E. H. Gombrich: A Problem of Method," in *Clues, Myths, and the Historical Method* (Baltimore, 1989), pp. 17–59.

67. *Schlangenritual*, p. 10.

68. "Schicksalsmächte im Spiegel antikisierender Symbolik," April 1924, Warburg Archive.

69. Notes to the 1927–28 Seminar on Method, Warburg Archive.

70. The German for "elective affinity" is the (now) Goethean "Wahlverwandtschaft." Warburg has, by this point in the essay, begun to preface "primitive" with "so-called." Walter Benjamin also relied on the concept of elective affinities to discuss transhistorical parallels. See Michael Löwy, "Sur le concept d'affinité élective," in *Rédemption et Utopie* (Paris, 1988), pp. 13–21 and passim.

71. See n. 3.

72. Warburg was aware of the Greek tradition of serpent symbolism as a symbolism of ambivalence, and he refers to the serpent's trait of shedding its skin as a symbol of rebirth. He also cites Jane Harrison, *Prolegomena to the Study of Greek Religion*, 3rd ed. (1922).

73. The letters from Warburg to Sachs, as well as some carbon copies of Sachs's letters, are in the archive of the William Hayes Fogg Museum, Harvard University Art Museums. I am grateful to Abby Smith for her assistance in the archive and to James Cuno, Director of the Harvard University Art Museums, for permission to cite the documents.

74. Unpublished memorandum, Warburg Archive.

75. Paul Sachs file, archive of the Fogg Museum.

76. Arnaldo Momigliano, "How Roman Emperors Became Gods," *American Scholar* 55 (Spring 1986): 181; reprinted in the *Ottavo Contributo alla Storia degli Studi Classici e del Mondo Antico* (Rome, 1987), p. 297; also in *On Pagans, Jews, and Christians* (Middletown, Conn., 1987), p. 92.

MICHAEL P. STEINBERG

www.ingramcontent.com/pod-product-compliance
Lightning Source LLC
Chambersburg PA
CBHW020321290526
45785CB00007B/2871